THE CALIFORNIA DOCUMENTATION HANDBOOK

A Guide for Supervisors, Peer Coaches, and Consulting Teachers

First Edition

January 2004

By

Frank Kemerer, John Crain and Catherine Maloney

Additional copies may be ordered directly from *Education Law Services*.
Call or fax your order to 877-966-6100.

NOTE: The information provided in this handbook is intended to be accurate and authoritative at the time of printing. The handbook is published and marketed with the understanding that neither the publisher nor the authors are rendering legal advice. If specific legal advice or assistance is required, the services of a competent professional should be sought. Readers should be aware that with the passage of time, some of the information contained in this handbook may become out of date.

FIRST EDITION

Education
Law Services™

3830 Valley Centre Drive • Ste. 705
PMB #174
San Diego, CA 92130
Phone / Fax: 877-966-6100

ISBN 0-9748768-0-1

TABLE OF CONTENTS

PREFACE

This handbook is addressed to school administrators, Peer Review and Assistance (PAR) consulting teachers, mentors for new teachers, peer coaches, teacher leaders, and others concerned with personnel decision making and teaching improvement. It differs from other materials on documentation in that it not only discusses the law and practice of documentation generally but also presents a comprehensive system of classroom documentation targeted to the teacher in need of assistance. California law and the No Child Left Behind Act require that all students are to become proficient on state assessments in the near future. As school districts and charter schools confront the challenges of improving student outcomes, they inevitably must concentrate on the quality and effectiveness of classroom teaching. The goal is to have a highly qualified teacher in every classroom. Thus, the needs of the teacher in need of assistance have become a high priority.

Chapter 1 provides an overview of employment law as it relates to California public school teachers, and Chapter 2 sets forth basic principles to be followed in investigating employee problems generally and writing letters of reprimand. Ensuing chapters take the discussion into the classroom. Chapter 3 discusses the characteristics of the teacher in need of assistance and what the implications are for supervision and consultation. Chapter 4 examines professional growth plan development and why it is important to link expected changes in teacher behavior to student performance.

Chapters 5 through 9 present a series of five focused observation instruments targeted to specific areas of teaching weakness that are designed to be used for periodic 15-30 minute classroom observations. Classroom walk-throughs are a critical component of a school's overall assessment system for marginally effective teachers. Each instrument is linked to one of the California Standards for the Teaching Profession, and in turn to the research on effective teaching. Standard Six is omitted from the discussion because it addresses developmental issues beyond the scope of classroom observation.

The instruments require little writing, thus enabling the evaluator to gather information easily and with confidence that it is related to accepted standards of teaching effectiveness. Each chapter illustrates how the instrument is to be completed in the context of a teacher in need of assistance. A sample follow-up memorandum also is presented for each instrument. Expected changes in teaching performance described in the memorandum are linked to effective teaching criteria and, if appropriate, to remediation activities and student performance.

Blank copies of the five focused observation instruments ready for use are contained in the first of five appendices. A template for the focused observation memorandum also is included in an appendix so that readers can construct them easily and systematically. Other appendices provide a list of generic remediation activities, the California Rules of Conduct of Professional Educators, and a comprehensive bibliography on effective teaching research.

We are indebted to several individuals for reading the initial manuscript draft and providing suggestions for improvement. They include Deberie Gomez, former Deputy Administrative Officer for Human Resources Services in the San Diego Unified School District; Diane Yerkes, Associate Professor of Educational Leadership at San Diego State University; Lionel "Skip" Meno, Dean of the College of Education at San Diego State University; Melinda Martin, Facilitator of the Educational Leadership Development Program (ELDA) at the University of San Diego; and Jose Gonzales, Assistant General Counsel for the San Diego Unified School District. We also are indebted to students in the ELDA program who provided feedback on several chapters and the use of our focused observation instruments during an all-day workshop on personal decision making. We much appreciate the helpful comments and suggestions from all these persons, as well as from individuals in the California Department of Education with whom we spoke, and absolve them all from any responsibility for the handbook's shortcomings.

We hope that the California school community will find this handbook useful in presenting strategies and techniques for effectively evaluating teachers, supporting their professional growth and improvement, and making informed and legally defensible personnel decisions.

CHAPTER ONE: THE LEGAL FRAMEWORK

While the focus of this handbook is the effective use of documentation to improve teaching practices and student outcomes, effective documentation also is essential to negative employment decisions when teachers fail to make the required changes or are incapable of meeting performance standards. The absence of sufficient documentation may seriously jeopardize a district's ability to remove an incompetent teacher and may increase the district's vulnerability to lawsuits. The documentation process we put forth in this handbook serves first and foremost the goal of fair treatment of school employees. Secondarily, it is meant to provide the rationale and supportive evidence to withstand legal challenges to the nonextension of contracts or contract termination.

With these goals in mind, it is first necessary to consider the legal framework that governs employment law and its implications for effective and legally permissible documentation practices. In this chapter we set forth the basics of employment law in California and in Chapter 2 we consider its implications for the process of documentation. Readers are advised that employment law is an intricate subject and that our discussion here is by no means exhaustive. More comprehensive sources are referenced throughout the chapter, and readers may wish to consult them and/or their district's attorney for more complete information.

As an illustration of many points we address, let's consider the case of Bob Instructor and Ima Leader:

> Bob is a forty-two-year-old veteran teacher in the Surfs Up Unified School District in Surfs Up, California. Bob has been on a permanent contract as a middle school social studies teacher in the district for fifteen years. Early in his career at Surfs Up, Bob had been active in union affairs, serving for a time as the local union representative on his campus. Prior to the November election, he was critical of his school principal, Ima Leader, for her directive that teachers remove all partisan political material from classrooms and not wear political campaign buttons while they teach. His letter complaining about the directive was published in the local newspaper. In the letter, he argued that the directive intrudes on the rights of teachers and runs counter to the role of the school in educating students about the importance of being politically involved. Aside from the letter, Bob has evidenced a certain casualness toward his professional responsibilities. Prior to the letter-writing incident, he had arrived late to school and left early on several occasions. More recently, he has been late to scheduled faculty meetings and failed to attend one meeting. His classroom instruction also has deteriorated to the point where Ima is really concerned about his value as a teacher.

> Now in her third year as principal at the middle school, Ima decides to tackle the letter-writing and the faculty meeting tardiness first. She considers both inappropriate and is considering sending Bob letters of reprimand. She wonders if she is on firm legal ground.

In the process of answering Ima's question, we will review the essentials of employment law and its implications for school administrators working to improve instruction and successfully address problems such as Ima is experiencing with Bob. We begin with a discussion of property rights and due process.

PROPERTY RIGHTS AND DISMISSAL

In 1972 the U.S. Supreme Court ruled that teachers have a protected property right in employment under the terms of the Fourteenth Amendment to the U.S. Constitution if the state gives them a "legitimate claim of entitlement" to it.[1] The Fourteenth Amendment provides in part that no state (or political subdivision of a state like a public school district) shall deprive a person of "life, liberty, or property, without due process of law." Thus, the dimensions of property rights in public employment are to be found in state law, local policies, collective bargaining agreements, and contractual provisions. Once a governmental entity has created a property right protected by the Fourteenth Amendment, it may not take that right away without providing the employee due process of law.

Employees who do not have property rights and are not protected by civil service rules or union contracts are said to be employed "at will." This means that they serve at the pleasure of the employer. For example, Educ. Code § 44953 states that substitute teachers may be dismissed at any time at the pleasure of the board. Since there is no expectation of continued employment in an at-will arrangement, the employee is not entitled to notice and a hearing before dismissal. Conversely, the employee need not give the employer any notice before quitting. The employment arrangement continues at the discretion of both parties. But as we shall see, there are some limitations on employer discretion to end an at-will arrangement.

Property Rights Under California Law

Under California law, full-time certificated teachers except those in very small districts must serve two consecutive school year probationary contracts before they can become permanent employees (see Figure 1-1). As probationary employees, they have an expectation of employment until the end of the first and the end of the second school year. Thus, a property right exists *during* the contract, and due process must be provided before a probationary teacher can be dismissed during the school year.

Figure 1-1   OVERVIEW OF CALIFORNIA TEACHER CONTRACTS*

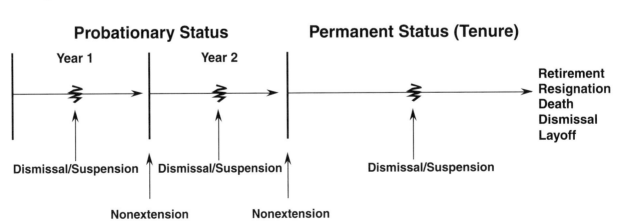

*Districts with more than 250 students

Conversely, the property right is over at the end of the first and again at the end of the second probationary year. Under Educ. Code § 44929.21, districts with more than 250 students can give notice to a second year probationary teacher that he/she will not be reelected for service for the following year, provided that notice of nonreelection is given by March 15. No specific notice date is given for not extending the first year probationary contract, but judicial decisions indicate that it would be unfair to wait until the last day of employment.[2] For the sake of uniformity, many districts follow the March 15 date for the first year as well.

No reasons need be stated with the notice, and no due process procedures are necessary. Governing boards cannot modify the two-year probationary period. Teachers must serve the full two years of probationary status,[3] and unions cannot negotiate due process protection for teachers at the end of the probationary contract years.[4] Does this mean that school administrators have full discretion in recommending contract nonextensions to the governing board? Not exactly, for reasons indicated below. But it seems fair to say that administrators and governing boards have considerable discretion to nonextend teacher contracts. This is of no value, however, to Ima Leader, since Bob is a permanent employee.

After serving two consecutive school year contracts, a probationary teacher chosen by the school board for a successive third year becomes classified as a permanent teacher at the beginning of that third year. Once elevated to permanent status, a teacher has a vested property right in employment within the scope of the teaching credential which tenure was conferred.[5] Permanent teachers can only be dismissed for grounds specified by statute and are afforded full due process rights. From a documentation standpoint, it is wise to consider the implication of the term "permanent." A teacher who has been permitted to ascend from probationary to permanent status is presumed to be effective. Thus, taking away the teacher's employment through dismissal should not be casually undertaken. School principals who embark on this path should realize that the effort may take several years and may well involve joint efforts with previous principals, as well as frequent consultation with the personnel director and school attorney.

The procedures are different for districts with fewer than 250 students. For these districts, probationary teachers can be given permanent status after three consecutive years or continued on a year-to-year basis thereafter, unless the district elects to dismiss probationary teachers during the school year for unsatisfactory performance (more about this later). In that instance, it must follow the same procedures for probationary teachers generally.

Permissible Grounds for Dismissal

The grounds for a dismissal of a probationary teacher during the school year or for dismissal of a permanent teacher at any time encompass reasons specified in Educ. Code § 44932. Among those listed are:

- immoral or unprofessional conduct
- dishonesty
- unsatisfactory performance

- evident unfitness for service

- physical or mental condition unfitting him or her to instruct or associate with children

- persistent violation of or refusal to obey the school laws of the state or reasonable regulations prescribed by the State Board of Education or the governing board

- conviction of a felony or any crime involving moral turpitude

- alcoholism or other drug abuse which makes the employee unfit to instruct or associate with children

Several of these warrant some explanation.

Immoral or Unprofessional Conduct

In the case of immoral or unprofessional conduct, it must be established that the conduct undermined the teacher's effectiveness. This was the thrust of the seminal ruling of *Morrison v. State Board of Education*, a decision of the California Supreme Court in 1969.[6] That case involved a teacher who had resigned when confronted with evidence of a private, consensual homosexual relationship. Though the relationship had not been known among students or teachers, the state revoked the teacher's credentials. The Court ruled in favor of the teacher, noting the absence of evidence that the relationship had negatively affected the teacher's performance.

Some years later, a California court of appeal was confronted with a case involving a sixth grade creative writing teacher who had continued to permit students to write derogatory stories about each other, contrary to administrative directives.[7] With regard to the charge of unprofessional conduct, the judges observed that, unlike the *Morrison* case, here there was evidence related to the teacher's classroom conduct to support the charge.

In recent years, the immoral conduct charge has extended to cases involving sexual harassment. In1994 a California court of appeal upheld use of the *Morrison* analysis to establish that a permanent teacher's persistent sexual harassment of students in his music classes rendered the teacher unfit to teach.[8]

Unsatisfactory Performance

The third reason – unsatisfactory performance – has received considerable attention in recent years in light of the movement toward uniform curriculum content standards and high stakes testing. For some time, California has required that school districts have a uniform system of evaluation and assessment of performance for all certificated employees. Since teachers are the focus of our attention here, we will focus our discussion on them. The school district may, with consent of the teacher union, include in its evaluation program any of the standards developed by the National Board for Professional Teaching Standards or any of the California Standards for the Teaching Profession (CSTP), if relevant to classroom performance (Educ. Code § 44661.5). Given the significance of the latter in teacher evaluation in this state, we have tailored the classroom focused observation instruments set forth in later chapters to these standards.

School districts are required to evaluate teacher performance as reasonably related to:

- Student achievement on grade level assessments and, if applicable, the state-adopted academic content standards as measured by state criterion-referenced assessments

- Instructional techniques and strategies

- Adherence to curricular objectives

- The establishment of a suitable learning environment

Hourly and temporary hourly certificated employees other than those employed in adult education classes are excluded from this process. Substitute teachers may be excluded at the discretion of the school district.

As delineated in Educ. Code §§ 44663-44664, a written report of the evaluation is to be given to the teacher not later than 30 days before the end of the school year, followed by a meeting between evaluator and teacher before the end of the school year. The teacher is entitled to respond in writing to the evaluation, and the response is to be included in the teacher's personnel file. Performance evaluation is required at least annually for probationary teachers; at least once every other school year for permanent teachers; and at least every five years for permanent teachers who have been employed at least ten years in the district, are highly qualified under NCLB standards, and whose previous evaluation was meets or exceeds standards, if the evaluator and teacher so agree. Performance deficiencies are to be accompanied by recommendations for improvement. If performance is so deficient as not to meet district standards, the teacher is to be notified in writing, and the supervisor thereafter must meet with the teacher to identify areas of deficiency and help the teacher improve. If the performance of a permanent teacher is rated as unsatisfactory under district standards, the teacher is to be evaluated annually until the teacher improves or is dismissed. Teachers whose teaching methods or instruction are unsatisfactory are to be referred to the Peer Assistance and Review (PAR) Program, if the district has instituted it.

A word about PAR (Educ. Code § 44500 and following sections). Enacted in 1999 as a replacement for the California Mentor Teacher Program, the California Peer Assistance and Review Program for Teachers is intended to assist in improving the performance of marginally effective or ineffective permanent teachers. Since dismissal of a permanent teacher is so difficult and stressful, PAR is intended to provide another option focused on improvement.[9] How successful it will be depends on many factors, including the willing support of the teacher union, the desire and ability of teachers to change their behavior, and the supervisory skills of both the consulting teacher and the principal. Consulting teachers are exemplary permanent teachers who serve as mentors to those needing assistance. It is to principals and consulting teachers that this handbook largely is addressed.

If a district and its teacher union elect to receive state funds to establish a PAR program,[10] the program must include the following principles:

- Permanent teachers (and probationary teachers in a district with fewer than 250 units of ADA) may volunteer to participate in or be referred to the program for unsatisfactory performance as evidenced in their evaluations. In addition, teachers may be referred pursuant to a collective bargaining agreement.

- Performance goals set for the participating teacher shall be in writing, clearly stated, and aligned with curricular objectives and student achievement.

- Multiple classroom observations are to be conducted.

- Enhancement of a cooperative relationship between the consulting teacher and the principal is to be encouraged.

- Staff development activities must be provided to assist the teacher improve.

- The PAR program is to be continuously monitored.

- The final evaluation of the teacher's participation in the program is to be placed in the teacher's personnel file.

The local PAR governance structure is to include a joint teacher-administrator panel that selects consulting teachers, reviews their peer review reports, makes recommendations to the governing board regarding participating teachers, and forwards to the governing board the names of those who are not able to perform satisfactorily after sustained assistance. The panel also is required to evaluate the PAR program annually and make recommendations as to the program's improvement to both the governing board and the union (Educ. Code § 44502).

The majority of a local PAR panel is to be composed of certificated teachers chosen by their peers. Administrative members are selected by the school district. The development and implementation of the program are to be negotiated with the district's teacher union, a fact which underscores the need both for cooperation and commitment by administrators and union leaders. Importantly, the statute states that the functions performed by bargaining unit members on behalf of the PAR process are not considered either management or supervisory activities (Educ. Code § 44503 (b)). This means that the school administration retains authority and responsibility to determine the status of a teacher in need of assistance or an ineffective teacher.

It is clear that remediation is behind the PAR process. Even the dismissal statute favors remediation. It requires the governing board or its authorized representative to send a teacher a 90-day written notice when the board contemplates dismissing the teacher on the grounds of unsatisfactory performance. The notice must be sufficiently specific to give the teacher an opportunity to correct the faults and overcome the grounds for the charge during this three-month period (Educ. Code § 44938 (b)). The written notice is to include the teacher's evaluation.

In short, unsatisfactory performance now requires extensive efforts to help the teacher in need of assistance or ineffective permanent teacher improve before moving toward a dismissal action. Hopefully, significant improvement will occur so as to make dismissal unnecessary.

Evident Unfitness for Service

The fourth reason for teacher dismissal, evident unfitness for service, has been the focus of some attention from courts. In a 1992 decision, a California court of appeal ruled that unfitness to teach does not mean the same thing as unprofessional conduct.[11] Rather, unfitness to teach encompasses a fixed character trait that is not remediable. This is so because unprofessional conduct requires a 45-day window for the employee to correct the faults and overcome the grounds for the charge. No such window is provided for evident unfitness to teach. In the case, the teacher had been charged with 29 specific acts of alleged unfitness for service. Most involved violent and occasionally profane outbursts against students and teachers over a period of time. Taken in the aggregate, the charges supported the teacher's dismissal.[12]

Persistent Violation of or Refusal to Obey School Laws or Reasonable Regulations

This reason for teacher dismissal is particularly relevant to documenting the teacher in need of assistance who has been on permanent status for a number of years. Reliance on several unsatisfactory evaluations likely will not be enough to overcome a legacy of prior good performance. To establish "persistent" violation of California school laws and/or reasonable regulations of the State Board of Education or governing board of the school district, administrators will have to spend considerable time in the classroom of the teacher in need of assistance gathering data. These data must then be converted into written form that indicates what it is that the teacher is doing wrong and what needs to be changed. Then future classroom walk-through observations will be needed to establish whether the teacher is improving or not. We will show in subsequent chapters how this can be done. If the teacher improves, then there will be no need for any disciplinary action. If the teacher does not improve, then the administrator may have the evidence to establish grounds for dismissal.

Note that this reason encompasses both violations of school laws and regulations developed by the State Board of Education, as well as the governing board of the school district. The regulations of the latter encompass board policies and administrative regulations. These are, in effect, the "law of the district," and can be grounds for dismissal if they are violated.

Be aware of a very important limitation in the state dismissal statute. Educ. Code § 44944 (a) specifies that no decision relating to the dismissal or suspension of a teacher shall be made based on charges or evidence of any nature relating to matters "occurring more than four years prior to the filing of the notice." Thus, administrators work within a four-year window in documenting the deficiencies of teacher in need of assistance.

California also has a set of Rules of Conduct for Professional Educators, the violation of which may result in revocation or suspension of the educator's credential. They are set forth in Title 5 of the California Code of Regulations. While the provisions of the code may not themselves be reasons for dismissal, they can be cited to add support to a case for dismissal of either teachers or administrators based on the statutory reasons previously discussed. Highlights of the rules are set forth here. They are reproduced in their entirety in Appendix B. Districts may add to these provisions through their own code of ethics.

- Professional candor and honesty required in letters and memoranda of employ-ment recommendation. [This rule specifically targets intentionally omitting key facts or including information the writer does not know to be true or knows to be false. It also precludes making unfounded positive comments to secure a resignation or buy off a threatened lawsuit. Not only is there an ethical responsibility to be honest, there is also a legal responsibility. In an important 1997 ruling, the California Supreme Court ruled that school officials who wrote letters of recommendation containing unreserved praise for a former school teacher and administrator who they knew had been involved in sexual misconduct with students can be subject to liability when the employee later engages in inappropriate sexual activity with a student. In this case, the letters recommended the former employee for any position without reservation or qualification, thus implying the administrator was fit to interact appropriately and safely with female students.[13]]

- Withdrawal from professional employment without good cause.

- Unauthorized private gain or advantage from use of confidential information relating to students or fellow professionals.

- Performance of duties when substantially mentally impaired for any reason, including alcohol or substance abuse. This rule also encompasses the assignment of such a person to perform duties.

- Harassment or retaliation against those who report actual or suspected wrongdoing.

- Failure to perform duties for a person because of discriminatory motives.

Impermissible Grounds for Dismissal

Up to this point, we have been talking about permissible reasons for taking away a teacher's property right in employment through a dismissal action. There are definitely some reasons we want to avoid. They fall into two general categories. The first involves the exercise of protected rights, and the second involves discrimination against a protected status.

Exercise of Protected Rights

At the top of the list of protected rights are those protected by the U.S. and California constitutions. Frequently, claims of retaliation for the exercise of free speech surface in dismissal actions. The First Amendment to the U.S. Constitution encompasses freedom of speech and press, as well as the rights of religious exercise and association. By virtue of a seminal 1968 U.S. Supreme Court decision, public employees, even those employed at-will, enjoy broad protection for expression in their role as citizens on matters of public interest, so long as (1) the statements are not made recklessly or with knowledge of their falsity, and (2) the statements do not impede either the school's functioning or the employee's performance.[14] Comments made in the employee's role as a citizen that concern the community interest are constitutionally protected. These might include a speech made to the PTA about alleged deficiencies in the English Language Learner program, a presentation to the school board about racial tension in the district, or statements on a radio talk show about the lack of student discipline in the school. However, according to the U.S. Supreme Court, remarks by public employees that do not concern a matter of public interest but relate to an employee's own personal interest are not constitutionally protected.[15]

Article I, section 2 of the California Constitution notes that every person may "freely speak, write and publish his or her sentiments on all subjects." Its language is very broad and sweeping, leading the California Supreme Court to rule that it is more protective of free speech than the First Amendment.[16] However, section 2 goes on to say that persons are "responsible for the abuse of this right." Thus, while complaints about one's own working conditions might be constitutionally protected under the state constitution when they wouldn't be under the federal constitution, if the remarks cause disruption or interfere significantly with the rights of others, they may lose their protection.

Bob Instructor's comments regarding a teacher's right to express political views in the classroom do not accurately reflect California law. In a case involving the San Diego Unified School District, a California court of appeal ruled that neither the protection accorded speech in the First Amendment to the U.S. Constitution, nor the protection found in Article I, section 2 of the California Constitution, limits the power of school authorities to dissociate themselves from political controversy by prohibiting employees from engaging in political advocacy in the instructional setting. Thus, partisan political activity such as petitions, posters, and the like can be restricted in the classroom and in the school's hallways unless the district provides otherwise. However, such is not the case when teachers are informally talking among themselves. As the court noted, "The relationship between co-employees has none of the elements of power and influence which exist between elementary and secondary school students and their instructors."[17] Even if Bob's views are in error, there is little question that they are constitutionally protected under both federal and state constitutional law. There simply is no evidence that Bob has abused his right of free speech. Thus, Ima Leader must not allow her frustration with Bob to prompt her to include references to the letter in her documentation of his deficiencies. Of course, if Bob were to fail to follow Ima's directive that he cease partisan political activity in the classroom, then his actions would warrant her sending him a letter of reprimand.

Because the California Constitution gives broader protection to free speech than does the federal constitution, we believe it is best not to distinguish between speech on matters of public concern and speech on matters relating to an employee's working conditions. All speech should be considered constitutionally protected. However, the *effect* of the expression is another matter. If speech is exercised in such a way as to undermine the teacher's effectiveness or damage the superior-subordinate relationship, it may have lost its protection and become grounds for a negative employment decision. Nevertheless, the burden of justification is very high. One can be sure that whenever claims of retaliation for the exercise of expression arise, the supporting documentation will be reviewed very carefully. The California Supreme Court has indicated that a teacher has a right to be heard on the claim that his dismissal for the exercise of constitutional rights was not justified by a compelling public interest.[18] To establish that a compelling public interest exists, the governing board must have convincing evidence of the abuse of protected rights. Given the tilt in the law toward protecting free speech, this is hard to do. Therefore, whenever possible, administrators should focus on something other than the exercise of a constitutional right. Even when a teacher can show that the exercise of a protected right played a substantial role in a negative employment decision, the U.S. Supreme Court has ruled that the school district can still prevail if it can show that it would have made the same decision in the absence of the exercise of the right.[19] The important lesson, then, is always to focus on *job-related deficiencies*.

Closely related to free speech is the constitutional right to associate with others. Encompassed within this right is the right to participate in union activities, a right that also is protected by the California Educational Employee Relations Act.[20] Recall in the scenario presented at the start of this chapter that Bob Instructor had served for a time as a union representative. Any hint by Ima Leader that Bob's deficiencies are somehow related to his involvement with the union would be unwise, to say the least. He may allege as much. But if there is no evidence, the allegation won't go far. In the case mentioned in the section on unprofessional conduct involving the dismissal of a creative writing teacher who allowed students in his classes to write derogatory stories, the California court of appeal noted that the teacher claimed his dismissal was related to his involvement in union affairs. However, there was no evidence to support the claim.

To what extent do California public school teachers enjoy a right to academic freedom in the classroom? Can they, for example, lead classroom discussion on controversial topics and be free from retaliation for doing so? Do they have the right to choose teaching materials and methodology? How about the right to award a grade to a student? Academic freedom is relatively undefined in both federal and California law. The U.S. Supreme Court has not heard a case directly involving the matter. While there are academic freedom cases in lower federal courts, most are decided against the teacher. In 1994 the California attorney general advised that he could find no judicial precedent "for the notion that a secondary teacher has a constitutional right to academic freedom."[21]

Public employees also have a Fourteenth Amendment liberty right to a good reputation. This liberty interest becomes implicated when the employer stigmatizes the employee's reputation and jeopardizes future employment opportunities.[22] Concern about intrusions on reputational rights is why administrators usually respond to press inquiries about a pending personnel matter with "no comment" or "you will need to check with the district's information office about that."

The California Legislature has conveyed by statute several rights to teachers related to our discussion. Included among them is the right to award grades, which can only be changed if the result of clerical error or mechanical mistake, fraud, bad faith, or incompetency (Educ. Code § 49066 (a)); the right to appear before a governing board (Educ. Code § 44040); and the right not to participate in personally intrusive surveys (Educ. Code § 49091.24). Disciplinary action cannot be taken against teachers who exercise these rights.

It is important to note that not only may a suspension or dismissal not be based on the exercise of protected rights, neither may a reassignment. As the California Supreme Court noted in a 1972 decision, "all administrative sanctions" involving protected rights require the showing of a compelling state interest.[23] In 1973 the California high court applied this rule to the transfer of a teacher who exercised First Amendment rights. As the court noted in that case, "Lesser penalties than dismissal can effectively silence teachers and compel them to forego exercise of the rights guaranteed them by our Constitution."[24] Thus, if Bob Instructor challenged Ima Principal's reassigning him to another position or seeking his transfer to another school over the letter-writing incident, he likely would be successful unless Ima can convincingly advance job-related reasons for the reassignment.

Discrimination Against a Protected Class

Employment decisions that violate federal and California civil rights laws also are impermissible. Here in capsule form are those most prominently related to employment in public schools.

Race. A federal law known as 42 United States Code (U.S.C.) § 1981 accords all persons the right to make and enforce contracts free from racial discrimination. The statute also prohibits discrimination occurring during the contract term. Penalties include both injunctive relief and compensatory damages.

Race, Religion, Sex. Title VII of the 1964 Civil Rights Act prohibits discrimination on the basis of race, color, religion, sex (including pregnancy), or national origin in all aspects of public and private employment in organizations with fifteen or more employees for each working day in each of twenty or more calendar weeks in the current or preceding year (42 U.S.C. §§ 2000 et seq.). Harassment on these grounds also is actionable under the statute. In addition to equitable relief such as back pay and reinstatement, the law allows monetary damages for intentional discrimination. The California Fair Employment and Housing Act (FEHA) is the state counterpart to Title VII. Under both Title VII and FEHA, the employee has to establish that he was subjected to some adverse employment action. This could encompass a discharge, reassignment, or demotion. A resignation also can trigger claims under these laws if the employee can show that working conditions had become so intolerable because of harassment that a reasonable person had no choice but to resign.

Disabilities. Section 504 of the Rehabilitation Act of 1973 prohibits discrimination on the basis of disability in any federally assisted program (29 U.S.C. § 794). A violation of the act results in sanctions including the loss of federal funding. The Americans with Disabilities Act (ADA) operates similarly to Section 504, but it applies more broadly and its remedies are greater (42 U.S.C. §§ 12101 et seq.). Title II of the ADA prohibits discrimination by a state or local governmental entity (including virtually all public and charter schools) against persons with disabilities and requires employers to make reasonable accommodation for persons with disabilities, once it is determined they can perform the job. Intentional violations of the ADA may result in the awarding of monetary damages.

Age. The Age Discrimination in Employment Act (ADEA) prohibits discrimination by employers, employment agencies, and unions in both public and private employment against employees aged forty or over unless age is a bona fide qualification reasonably necessary to carry out job responsibilities (29 U.S.C. §§ 621 et seq.). Penalties for violating the ADEA are similar to those for Title VII.

Sexual Orientation. The California Fair Employment and Housing Act (FEHA) encompasses sexual orientation. Specifically, this law makes it an unlawful employment practice for employers, employment agencies, and unions to discriminate on the basis of race, religious creed, color, national origin, ancestry, physical disability, mental disability, medical condition, marital status, sex, age, or sexual orientation. Harassment on these grounds may provide cause for a claim under this law. Victims can file suit in state court under FEHA and recover damages.

DUE PROCESS REQUIREMENTS

Due process of law has two dimensions, substantive and procedural. Substantive due process refers to the basis for the decision and is commonly known as "just cause." From the documentation perspective, just cause means the presence of clear and convincing reasons supported by sufficient evidence to warrant taking away a person's constitutionally protected property right in employment. We discussed reasons for dismissal in the previous section.

Here we review procedural due process to get a sense of what California law requires. It is important to note that the matter is quite complex and only an overview is provided. School leaders are advised to check the relevant statutes, local policy, and the union contract carefully. While unions cannot alter state law governing the dismissal of teachers, they can and usually do negotiate procedures for disciplinary action short of dismissal.

Probationary teachers may be dismissed during the year for unsatisfactory performance or for any of the reasons listed in Educ. Code § 44932 in accordance with the following due process procedures (for the procedures in districts with less than 250 students, see § 44948.5).[25] Remember that the only due process requirement for nonextension of a probationary teacher's contract at the end of the second year is notice by March 15. No specific date is given for nonextension of a first year probationary teacher's contract. The following chart presents the procedures that apply to the dismissal for cause of a probationary teacher during the school year. All references are to the California Education Code.

Figure 1-2

Steps to Dismiss for Cause – Probationary Teacher

Step One: Notice of Intent to Dismiss (Educ. Code § 44948.3)
<ul><li>Superintendent or designee gives 30 days prior written notice of intent to dismiss.</li><li>Notice given not later than March 15 for second year probationary teachers.</li><li>The notice shall include the reasons for the dismissal and notice of an opportunity to appeal. If unsatisfactory performance is the reason, a copy of the evaluation is to be included.</li><li>Governing board may opt for specific time of suspension without pay in lieu of dismissal.</li></ul>

Step Two: Hearing (Educ. Code § 44948.3)

- The teacher has 15 days to submit a written request for a hearing. Failure to make a request constitutes a waiver of the hearing.
- The board may hold the hearing itself or seek appointment of an administrative law judge to conduct the hearing and provide a recommendation to the governing board.
- The governing board makes its decision based on substantial evidence.

Step Three: Appeal

- Teacher has the option of challenging the board's administrative decision in California court.

The procedures for dismissing a permanent teacher are more elaborate. This should not be surprising, in that the permanent teacher has had two years of probationary status. The assumption is that once elevated to permanent status, a permanent teacher's contract should not be taken away easily. California courts interpret these provisions strictly with the goal of assuring fairness.[26]

Figure 1-3

Steps to Dismiss for Cause – Permanent Teacher

Step One: Written charges filed with governing board (Educ. Code §§ 44934, 44938)

- Person signs and verifies, or governing board formulates, written charges of grounds for dismissal or suspension without pay as specified in Educ. Code §§ 44932 or 44933. Teachers may be suspended only for unprofessional conduct. Teacher unions may negotiate the terms and conditions for suspensions up to 15 days (Govt. Code § 3543.2 (b)).

- If charges of unprofessional conduct, teacher must be given written notice that he has at least 45 days to improve before any action on charges will be taken.

- If unsatisfactory performance, teacher must be given written notice that he has at least 90 days to improve before action on charges taken. The notice must include the teacher evaluation. Governing board may act during the time period composed of the last one-fourth of the school days it has scheduled for computing apportionments in any fiscal year if, prior to the time period, the teacher has received written notice of unsatisfactory performance, including the teacher evaluation.

- For both unprofessional conduct and unsatisfactory performance, notice must be sufficiently specific to enable the teacher to correct the faults and overcome grounds for charges.

Step Two: Governing board gives notice of intent to dismiss or suspend (Educ. Code §§ 44934, 44936, 44937)

- Governing board decides by majority vote whether to dismiss or suspend without pay at the end of 30 days from the date of service of the notice. The notice cannot be served on the teacher between May 15 and September 15.

- Charges of unprofessional conduct or unsatisfactory performance must be sufficiently specific so teacher can prepare a defense. The statutes and rules the teacher is alleged to have violated must be stated, as well as the facts relevant to the charges.

- If no hearing requested, teacher is dismissed or suspended without pay at expiration of the 30-day period.

Step Three: Hearing (Educ. Code §§ 44943, 44944, 44945)

- If teacher requests a hearing, the governing board has the option either of rescinding its intention to dismiss or suspend or of scheduling a hearing.

- The hearing must be held within 60 days from the date of the request.

- The process now takes on the formality of preparation for a civil trial, with a formal accusation required from the board and, within 30 days thereafter, the exercise of discovery rights by both parties. Oral depositions may occur after this time frame.

- The hearing is conducted by the Commission on Professional Competence (CPC) composed of a member selected by the teacher, a member selected by the governing board, and an administrative law judge. The law judge serves as chairperson.

- The CPC determines by majority vote whether or not the teacher should be dismissed in a dismissal case, or whether or not the teacher should be suspended (and the period of suspension) in a suspension case.[27]

Step Four: Appeal

- On petition by either party, the decision of the CPC may be reviewed by a court.
- The court exercises independent judgment on the evidence.

It is not permissible to fire a public employee who has a property right and then "cure" any due process defect by providing notice of reasons and a hearing after the fact.[28] Nor is it permissible simply to suspend a probationary or permanent employee without pay pending a full due process dismissal hearing.[29] Thus, even the temporary loss of a state-conveyed property right requires a due process hearing under California law.[30] Pursuant to Govt. Code § 3543.2 (b), school districts may negotiate causes and procedures for disciplinary action short of contract nonextension and teacher dismissal, including suspensions without pay up to 15 days, with the teacher union. Thus, it is important to check the union contract before undertaking teacher discipline.

This concludes our discussion of the legal framework structuring teacher employment in California. Readers are reminded that employment law is a complex subject and that our discussion here is by no means complete. Administrators are well advised to consult with school district attorneys if they are uncertain about the law or its implications for campus-level decision making. With this in mind, we now turn to the process of effective documentation and consider how the legal framework affects it.

REFERENCES

1. Board of Regents v. Roth, 408 U.S. 564 (1972).
2. Grimsley v. Board of Trustees, 235 Cal. Rptr. 85 (Cal. App. 5 Dist. 1987). In a footnote, the appellate court observed that waiting until June 29 to notify a probationary employee that his/her employment would end on June 30 "might well be deemed unreasonable, particularly where the teacher could show reliance upon satisfactory performance evaluations from the district in not seeking other employment." The court added, "We cannot imagine a school district giving such short notice of its determination of nonretention to a first year probationary teacher."
3. Fleice v. Chualar Union Elementary School District, 254 Cal. Rptr. 54 (Cal. App. 6 Dist. 1988).
4. Board of Education of Round Valley Unified School District v. Round Valley Teachers Association, 52 Cal. Rptr.2d 115 (Cal. 1996).
5. However, the property right does not encompass a specific teaching assignment. Adelt v. Richmond School District, 58 Cal. Rptr. 151 (Cal. App. 1 Dist. 1967).
6. Morrison v. State Board of Education, 82 Cal. Rptr. 175 (Cal. 1969). The Court delineated seven criteria to be used in assessing whether or not immoral or unprofessional conduct has such an effect. These are known as the Morrison factors. They include: (1) the likelihood that the conduct may have adversely affected students or fellow teachers, (2) the degree of such adversity anticipated, (3) the proximity or remoteness in time of the conduct, (4) the type of teaching certificate held by the party involved, (5) the extenuating or aggravating circumstances, if any, surrounding the conduct, (6) the likelihood of the recurrence of the questioned conduct, and (7) the extent to which disciplinary action may inflict an adverse impact or chilling effect upon the constitutional rights of the teacher involved or other teachers.
7. Powers v. Bakersfield City School District, 204 Cal. Rptr. 185 (Cal. App. 5 Dist. 1984).
8. Governing Board of ABC Unified School District v. Haar, 33 Cal. Rptr.2d 744 (Cal. App. 2 Dist. 1994).
9. For an enthusiastic description from a variety of perspectives of the potential for PAR to improve teacher performance, see Gary Bloom and Jennifer Goldstein (eds), The Peer Assistance and Review Reader (The New Teacher Center, UC-Santa Cruz, 2000). Two chapters that are particularly insightful are "Intervening with a Veteran Teacher in Trouble" by mentoring teacher Wendy Baron and "Susan's Story" by Linda St. John, who writes about the mentee's experience. Two other chapters that are instructive are "Peer Assistance and Review: Enhancing What Teachers Know and Can Do" by Julia Koppich and "Peer Assistance and Review: Potential and Pitfalls" by Arthur Costa and Robert Garmston.
10. It is clear that the legislature wants school districts to participate. The statute provides that districts choosing not to participate in the program are ineligible for funding for other programs such as the Administrator Training and Evaluation Program. Beginning February 2002, districts that choose not to participate must explain their decisions at an annual governing board meeting. Educ. Code § 44504 (c).
11. Woodland Joint Union School District. Commission on Professional Competence, 4 Cal. Rptr.2d 227 (Cal. App. 3 Dist. 1992).
12. The teacher in the Woodland case had tried to argue that each of the 29 reasons should have been assessed independently against the unfitness for service standard. The appellate court responded with this colorful comment: "When a camel's back is broken, we need not weigh each straw in its load to see which one could have done the deed."
13. Randi W. v. Muroc Joint Unified School District, 60 Cal. Rptr.2d 263 (Cal. 1997). To avoid liability, the court noted that employers can either write a full disclosure letter or a "no comment" letter that reveals only employment history. With regard to the former, the justices noted that as long as the information is based on credible evidence and made without malice upon request of a prospective employer, the writer is entitled to a qualified privilege from defamation suits under California law. Cal. Civil Code § 47 (c).
14. Pickering v. Board of Education, 393 U.S. 563 (1968).
15. Connick v. Myers, 461 U.S. 138 (1983).
16. Robins v. Pruneyard Shopping Center, 153 Cal. Rptr.2d 854 (Cal. 1979), aff'd, 447 U.S. 74 (1980).
17. California Teachers Association v. Governing Board of San Diego Unified School District, 53 Cal. Rptr.2d 474 (Cal. App. 4 Dist. 1996), p. 481.
18. Bekiaris v. Board of Education, 100 Cal. Rptr. 16 (Cal. 1972).
19. Mt. Healthy City School District v. Doyle, 429 U.S. 274 (1977).
20. Cal. Govt. Code §§ 3540 et seq.
21. 77 Ops Atty Gen. 204 (1994). The attorney general had been asked whether a teacher may refuse to present material relating to the district's abstinence-based sex education program based on an academic freedom clause in the school district's collective bargaining contract. The answer was no. A collective bargaining contract cannot contravene the authority of the state and the district to determine the content of courses and curriculum.

22. However, the U.S. Supreme Court has ruled that stigmatizing by public officials unaccompanied by any loss of status does not trigger a Fourteenth Amendment liberty right violation. Serious stigmatizing, however, might constitute an invasion of personal privacy under state law. Paul v. Davis, 442 U.S. 693 (1976)

23. Bekiaris v. Board of Education, 100 Cal. Rptr. 16 (Cal. 1972).

24. Adcock v. San Diego Unified School District, 109 Cal. Rptr. 676 (Cal. 1973), p. 680.

25. In 2002 a California court ruled that the dismissal provisions apply to probationary teachers holding emergency permits in the same manner as to those holding regular certification. Regan v. Governing Board of Sonora Union High School District, 2002 WL 31009412 (Cal. App. 5 Dist., Sept. 6, 2002) unpublished.

26. For example, in 1999 the California Supreme Court ruled that Educ. Code § 44944(e) is unconstitutional by imposing one-half the cost of the administrative law judge in a commission termination hearing on the teacher who does not prevail, since this has the effect of denying due process by deterring cost-conscious teachers from challenging their terminations. Calif. Teachers Assoc. v. State, 84 Cal. Rptr.2d 425 (Cal. 1999).

27. In a dismissal case, the California Supreme Court ruled that the CPC may not decide that a lesser punishment is warranted. Fontana Unified School District v. Burman, 246 Cal. Rptr. 733 (Cal. 1988).

28. Cleveland Board of Education v. Loudermill, 470 U.S. 532 (1985).

29. The California Supreme Court ruled in Skelly v. State Personnel Board, 124 Cal. Rptr. 14 (Cal. 1985), that pre-removal safeguards "must include notice of the proposed action, the reasons therefor, a copy of the charges and materials upon which the action is based, and the right to respond either orally or in writing to the authority initiating the imposing discipline." This is commonly known as a "Skelly hearing" after the name of the case. The court noted that post-removal safeguards do nothing to protect the employee who is wrongfully disciplined against the temporary deprivation of property.

30. The U.S. Supreme Court later interpreted the U.S. Constitution differently in a 1997 ruling. Gilbert v. Homar, 520 U.S. 924 (1997). However, the Gilbert decision deals only with federal constitutional issues, not matters of state law.

CHAPTER TWO: THE PRACTICE OF DOCUMENTATION

Administrators seem to assume that "everything should be documented." We disagree. What is important in our view is the *quality* of written documentation, not the quantity. Too much paperwork in a personnel file often is a sign of poor documentation. Too little is a sign that the underpinnings for a negative employment decision have not been firmly established. Administrators need to apply the "Goldilocks test" – not too much, not too little, but just right. How can this be done? Here we sketch the basics, drawing upon our scenario involving Bob Instructor presented in the previous chapter.[1]

ORAL DIRECTIVES

First, relatively minor matters can be handled most effectively by oral directives. This is particularly true of beginning teachers, who look to their principals as mentors. If every misstep is "written up," the working relationship will be compromised. Oral directives should be followed up with notes to the file, which serve as memory joggers. The chief value of a note to the file is that its contents can be utilized later in constructing a letter of reprimand in the face of repeated failures to follow directives.

But suppose a teacher requests to see the informal notes that the administrator has made about him. Should the administrator hand them over? Certainly. We strongly endorse a very simple maxim in personnel decision making:

NO SECRETS, NO SURPRISES

The purpose of documentation is not to entrap. The purpose is to assure that personnel decisions are fair. Accordingly, everything an administrator writes down, even an informal note to the file that is not intended for anyone other than the maker, should be written in such a way that there would be no embarrassment if the note were posted on the Internet. The same is true of e-mail communiques, which often find their way to any number of audiences. Always stick to the facts.

With regard to Bob Instructor, let's assume that Ima Leader decided that the best way to handle Bob's arriving late to school and leaving early was to talk with him informally about it. Doing so, she hoped, would preserve the employer-employee relationship. As a new principal, Ima wants to earn the respect of her veteran teachers. Keeping the communication friendly and informal, she rightly believes, has the best chance of preserving the working relationship. She listened to Bob's excuse and gently reminded him of the necessity to be present during school hours. Ima made a note to the file regarding the date and substance of her conversation with Bob. Here is the note that she made:

> 10/22/01 Spoke with Bob Instructor about leaving school early last Friday and arriving 40 minutes late yesterday and 30 minutes late today. Bob said he is

trying to complete a sailboat he is building in time for a race later this month. He said he would not leave early or be late again unless he checked with me first.

After her conversation with Bob, the problem disappeared. The note to the file was retained in accord with district policy. Collective bargaining agreements also should be reviewed to determine if they have provisions relating to progressive discipline.

LETTER OF REPRIMAND

More formal written documentation should be considered only (1) when the teacher is not responding to oral directives, resulting in a pattern of behavior that must be corrected or (2) the teacher has failed to follow board policy or written directives in a significant way. In either of these situations, the administrator needs to construct a letter of reprimand and share it with the teacher. Note that some districts may require one or more intermediate steps before a letter of reprimand is sent. Such a form of progressive discipline may begin with a verbal warning, then progress to a written warning, and then to a formal letter of reprimand. Make sure that you are following the policies and collective bargaining agreements of your district. Generally, a letter of reprimand will have these characteristics, which we call the essential elements of a letter of reprimand:

- Written on school stationery so that is official.
- Includes the date when it was written.
- Describes the nature of the allegation and the nature of the investigation if one was required, the dates and times of specific incidents, and the dates when the administrator spoke with the teacher about the matter.
- Sets forth findings of fact resulting from the investigation.
- States conclusions regarding what happened and which laws, policies, administrative directives, or union contract provisions were violated and what impact the acts may have had on others.
- Issues specific directives regarding expected future conduct, including any remedial activities the teacher is to undertake.
- Offers the teacher an opportunity to respond within a specified time period.
- Includes the dated signature of the teacher, or if the teacher refuses to sign, the signature of a third party witness that the teacher received the memorandum.

These characteristics need to be altered somewhat when the matter relates to classroom deficiencies. We will show how to do this in subsequent chapters.

Notice how the components of the memorandum flow from one to the other. The first major component, and the most important, is the investigation. If the investigation is poorly done, then the entire documentation process will be undermined. The administrator will not have a full understanding of the facts surrounding the problem and thus may reach the wrong conclusion. The directives that stem from the conclusion will not be effective in correcting the problem and, worse, may give the teacher's representative the opportunity to turn the tables against the administration by challenging the ability of the principal to document effectively.

School administrators often ask us whether it is possible to utilize incidents occurring in past years to establish a pattern of teacher ineffectiveness or wrongdoing. Generally, we have said that if the matter is relevant to a contemporary concern, it would be appropriate to incorporate it in documentation. But remember that the California dismissal statute specifies that charges or evidence cannot extend beyond the previous four years. Even within this time span, it seems only fair to avoid citing previous incidents that have been corrected. Assume, for example, that a teacher had a several instances of arriving late to school during the teacher's first year of employment and was issued a written directive to arrive on time or face possible nonextension of the teacher's probationary contract at the end of the year. For the next two years, the teacher never was late. Then the teacher failed to attend a scheduled in-service without a valid excuse. Citing the prior lateness episode in documentation would not be appropriate because it has no relationship to the current incident and, indeed, never recurred after the directive had been issued. In effect, the teacher complied with the lateness directive, and the matter remains closed. New discipline cannot be issued for conduct for which the teacher previously has been disciplined.

WRITING A LETTER OF REPRIMAND

Ima Leader hoped that she could remedy Bob Instructor's being late to faculty meetings by talking informally with him, just as she had done earlier regarding his attendance. But such was not the case. Though Bob ceased partisan political activity in the classroom, he has remained resentful. At one point, he told Ima that he felt the faculty meetings were a waste of his time and that he would not attend. Ima gently reminded Bob that the meetings were scheduled in compliance with the collective bargaining contract and that his attendance was obligatory unless he had a valid excuse. Bob greeted this reminder with stony silence. His attendance at the meetings continued to be sporadic.

Ima has decided that she cannot condone Bob's absence any longer. She scheduled a formal conference with him. At the conference, she relied on her notes to the file to point out that he had been late for or left early at three faculty meetings and failed to attend the most recent meeting. She reminded Bob after each of the incidents, and she had talked with him about the need to be on time. In response, Bob reiterated that he failed to see the need to attend the meetings since most of the topics did not concern him and he had better ways to spend his time. Ima concluded the conference by telling Bob that he left her no alternative but to write him a letter of reprimand.

Here is the letter that she wrote, drawing in part on her previous notes to the file and on her conference with Bob. Notice how the letter conforms to the characteristics of an effective letter of reprimand previously set forth. Notice how she anchors her conclusions in district practice and the relevant provision of the collective bargaining contract. Doing so adds credibility to her directive. Note as well that she avoids any mention of Bob's commentary published in the local newspaper criticizing her earlier directive about ceasing partisan political activity in class. Had she done so, Bob would immediately have a basis for claiming retaliation for the right of free speech.

ESSENTIAL ELEMENTS	**SURFS UP MIDDLE SCHOOL**
Letterhead Stationery	Surfs Up Unified School District

Date

May 22, 2003

TO: Bob Instructor
FROM   Ima Leader, Principal
RE: Faculty Meetings

Allegation

During the past semester, you have failed to attend the regularly scheduled faculty meetings in timely fashion. Specifically:

Findings of Fact

- You were 25 minutes late to the faculty meeting held at 3:30 P.M. on Friday, February 14. When I spoke with you about this after the meeting, you indicated that you had papers that needed to be corrected before the weekend when you would be out of town. I explained that I really didn't think correcting papers was a good reason not to be in attendance.
- You left half way through the faculty meeting held at 3:30 P.M. on March 7. When I spoke with you about your leaving early, you said that you didn't find the discussion of relevance to you, so you left. I notified you both orally and in writing that I didn't find your excuse valid.
- You were 15 minutes late to the faculty meeting held at 3:30 P.M. on Friday, April 11. When I asked you about your lateness and reminded you that I had requested that you be prompt following the earlier episodes, you simply shrugged your shoulders and walked away.
- You failed to attend the faculty meeting held at 3:30 P.M. on Friday, May 16.

When we met in my office on Tuesday, May 20, at 3:30 to discuss this matter, you said that the meetings are, in your words, "a waste of time" and you see no reason to attend them.

Conclusions

Your failure to attend the faculty meetings in timely fashion is a violation of my administrative directive and of Article 4, section 2 of the collective bargaining contract that recognizes the right of school principals to schedule monthly faculty meetings within the 40 hour work week.

Directive

In the future, I expect you to attend all regularly scheduled faculty meetings. If you find that you will arrive late, leave early, or not be in attendance at all, please state the reasons in writing to me prior to the meeting. I reserve the right to approve or disapprove them.

I hope that we can work together as colleagues in the best interest of our students. It is in this spirit that I welcome your attendance and participation in our professional deliberations.

Copy: Personnel File

Opportunity to Respond

I have received a copy of this letter. I understand that my signature does not necessarily indicate that I agree with its contents. I further understand that I have a right to respond within ten working days if I disagree.

Dated Signature

/s/ _____ Date _____
          Bob Instructor

The importance of the opportunity to respond portion cannot be overemphasized. Educ. Code § 44031 provides that negative information cannot be placed in an employee's file unless the employee has first been notified and given an opportunity to comment on the information. If this is not done, then the negative information cannot be used later against the employee. This statutory right has been construed by the California Supreme Court to apply not just to derogatory information destined for the personnel file but to derogatory information that could affect the person's employment status wherever it is kept.[2] This emphasizes again the importance of the maxim "No secrets, no surprises."

If Bob's response to the letter of reprimand reveals new information that Ima did not consider, then Ima will have the opportunity to reopen her investigation. Based on the new information, she may decide that her original conclusions were wrong. If so, she has the opportunity to correct the letter of reprimand or even withdraw it. Better to do this now than later when Bob prevails in a challenge through district or union-negotiated contract avenues of redress. If Bob's response offers nothing new, then Ima should acknowledge this fact in a brief reply memo and place both Bob's response and her reply memo in his personnel file. If Bob continues the exchange, Ima is best off not being drawn into it, lest she lose both her objectivity and her credibility. The repetitive nature of Bob's responses, coupled with their tone, may by themselves be enough to convince a school board member or member of a commission on professional competence, if it comes to that, that Ima was right all along.

Suppose Bob does not respond within the specified time period. If there is no response, then it can be assumed that Bob accepts the letter of reprimand. It will not be very convincing for Bob or his representative to claim months later when a notice of suspension or dismissal is pending that the letter was a tissue of lies. If so, why hadn't he taken advantage of the opportunity to respond?

Finally, always check both district policy and the collective bargaining contract to make sure that your progressive discipline actions are in accord with these documents. Pay particular attention to time lines, since they can be easily overlooked.

POINTERS ON CONDUCTING INVESTIGATIONS

As we noted above, the investigatory phase of documentation is the most important. But administrators often have trouble knowing exactly how to conduct an investigation. Here are some quick pointers. While we are focusing on teachers in this handbook, the observations made here apply to investigations of employees generally.

First, do not delay in beginning an investigation into either alleged teacher wrongdoing or ineffectiveness. Some administrators assume that if persons who witness events are unwilling to prepare a statement or step forward to testify, nothing can be done. While it is true that teachers have a right to confront witnesses against them at a due process hearing, nothing precludes an administrator from beginning an investigation. Where there are rumors, there may be truth. When contemplating an investigation, keep in mind that others may need to be involved too. The personnel director always should be informed when allegations against a teacher or other employee surface that might trigger an investigation. Claims of employee sexual harassment or abuse against students will necessarily involve the Title IX coordinator. When matters are potentially serious, the school attorney will need to be involved and actually may direct the investigation. This is most likely to be true when complaints also have been filed with law enforcement or outside administrative agencies. In such cases, it will be necessary to contact them to coordinate efforts and to assert the school district's obligations, such as maintaining confidentiality of records, safeguarding privacy rights of students, and protecting the professional reputation of employees.

When students are victims of alleged employee wrongdoing, do not delay in alerting their parents. This is particularly true in the context of sexual harassment and abuse. When students are victims of alleged employee wrongdoing, it is better to have parents as partners in the investigation than for them to learn later on about wrongdoing involving their child. If the wrongdoing consists of child abuse under California law, the events must be reported to the appropriate law enforcement agency.

If a complaint has been registered against an employee, ask complainants separately to fill out and sign a complaint form, describing the nature of the alleged wrongdoing and identifying other witnesses. Follow up with an interview to ascertain the credibility of the allegation. Do not promise confidentiality because some of the information in an investigatory file may have to be released to third parties under the California Public Records Act and because the accused may have the right to confront accusers if formal action is taken.

Interview student and employee witnesses separately. Follow a set of questions prepared in advance and targeted toward what you want to learn. Have witnesses complete and sign a statement in their native language. Again, do not promise confidentiality. Make sure that your investigatory procedure is in accord with district policy and practice. Consult district officials or the school attorney if in doubt.

Interview the accused, following the same procedures used when interviewing witnesses. Do not assume guilt. Treat the accused in the same manner you treat the complainants and witnesses. To avoid future allegations of a coerced resignation, ensure that resignations are informed and voluntary. Consult the district's personnel office or school attorney before taking any action on either matter.

Be careful about disclosing information. Provisions of state law prevent the disclosure of information about the victims of crimes. Additionally, the right to privacy is an inalienable right under Article I, section 1 of the California Constitution and encompasses both adults and minors.[3] Because the law in this area is complex, it is difficult to know when to disclose and when not to. For this reason, we believe administrators are better off deferring to the judgments of those district officials who know what the law is. In addition, the Family Educational Rights and Privacy Act (FERPA) prevents disclosure of personally identifiable information about students and families to third parties without parent permission. In the absence of authorization, remove personally identifiable student information from witness statements and other documentary evidence, including memoranda when they are released to third parties in conformity with the

California Public Records Act, which tilts toward disclosure. There are exceptions to nondisclosure in FERPA, the most important of which for our purposes is legitimate educational interest. In the chapters of this handbook dealing with classroom documentation, we do include the first names of students in memoranda directed to the teacher because the teacher, the principal, and, where involved, the consulting teacher need to know the identity of students who are not being taught effectively. Later, this information will be deleted if the memoranda are used for other purposes.

Be cautious in communicating with the news media because student and family privacy rights and employee constitutional and contractual rights may be involved. Use prepared statements, preferably handled by the district communication office. Remember that nothing is ever "off the record."

Finally, when the investigation is over, retain the documentation file supporting the disciplinary action for possible future use. Where it is stored varies. In some instances, the file is kept with the school attorney. In others, the file is kept in the personnel office or the superintendent's office. In any case, it is not advisable to place the documentation file in the teacher's personnel file kept in the personnel department because of (1) the possibility of reprisal, (2) the provision of the California Education Code that gives teachers the right to challenge information contained in their personnel file, (3) the difficulty of excising personally identifiable information under FERPA, and (4) the potential damage to the teacher from portions of the investigatory file that are false or misleading. The only documents that should be stored in the central personnel department file should be the recommendation for discipline, the formal disciplinary charges, and the documents reflecting the disposition of the discipline charges.

Under California law, personnel records are considered permanent records and are to be retained indefinitely.[4] Derogatory information becomes part of the permanent record only after the time for filing a grievance has passed or the information has been sustained by the grievance process.

CONCLUSION: TEN KEYS TO SUCCESSFUL DOCUMENTATION

Here are ten important lessons to be learned about effective documentation.

- **Don't delay.** If the matter appears to be important, begin the documentation process soon. If you delay, the message is conferred that you really didn't consider it very important.

- **Investigate, confer, write - in that order.** Remember that the investigation is the most important part of the documentation process because the conclusions you reach and the directives you give are dependent upon them.

- **Focus on job-related deficiencies.** Avoid legally impermissible bases for negative employment decisions.

- **Follow district policy, collective bargaining contracts, and specified time lines scrupulously.** Check these documents periodically to make sure you are adhering to them.

- **Avoid acting when angry.** Take time to think through how you will respond to a matter that concerns you. Act rationally and objectively.

- **Remember that the school board is a political body.** Politicians want to get reelected. It will not be politically wise for a school board member to back a dismissal recommendation that is not well documented.

- **Avoid inflammatory, sexist, and racist language.** There is no need to inflame a teacher to the point where the teacher seeks vengeance.

- **Assume your e-mail and hard copy communiques will be widely distributed and read.** In effect, you are publishing when you write. Make sure the words are spelled correctly, the style is appropriate, and the tone is unemotional. If in doubt, have an administrative colleague edit what you write.

- **Treat all employees alike.** Treat those you like in the same way you treat those you don't like.

- **Keep it simple.** One or two pages should suffice for a letter of reprimand. Edit out extraneous material and get to the point.

Underlying effective documentation is a very simple proposition: Do unto others as you would have them do unto you.

REFERENCES

1. Since this handbook is concerned primarily with classroom documentation, here we only provide an overview of the principles of documentation in general. For a more detailed discussion, see Steven J. Andelson, FRISK Documentation Model (1998). *See also* Kelly Frels and Janet Horton, A Documentation System for Teacher Improvement or Termination, Fifth Edition, Education Law Association (2003).
2. Miller v. Chico Unified School District, 175 Cal. Rptr. 72 (Cal. 1979).
3. American Academy of Pediatrics v. Lungren, 66 Cal. Rptr.2d 210 (Cal. 1997) (statute requiring minor to secure parental consent or judicial authorization before obtaining an abortion violates the minor's right of privacy under the California Constitution).
4. California Administrative Code, title 5, § 16023.

CHAPTER THREE: THE TEACHER IN NEED OF ASSISTANCE

In a time of increased accountability for student achievement, many educators are concerned about the teacher who needs assistance. The supervisory strategies used with this teacher are often different from those used with the teacher who is consistently ineffective or willfully fails to follow recommendations for improvement. With the teacher in need of assistance, the primary goal is to assist and support the teacher's improvement. Assistance and support for struggling teachers is the central thrust of the legislation that implemented the Beginning Teacher Support and Assessment (BTSA) Program in 1997 and the Peer Assistance and Review (PAR) Program in 1999. Given California's emphasis on remediation and support for teachers experiencing difficulties, school administrators are well advised to develop the supervisory skills that will allow them to effectively motivate and support improved teaching practices in the teachers they supervise. If reasonable improvement does not occur, supervisors must demonstrate that remediation and support have been provided if they choose to recommend contract nonextension for a probationary teacher or contract termination of a permanent teacher.

The purpose of this handbook is to provide administrators, peer coaches, consulting teachers, and others with the necessary tools to facilitate improved classroom instruction, better professional practice and increased student achievement. In this chapter, we focus on identifying some of the sources of teachers' poor instructional performance and the skills supervisors and consulting teachers need in order to facilitate improvement.

THE SOURCES OF MARGINAL TEACHER PERFORMANCE

The Association for Supervision and Curriculum Development (ASCD) handbook entitled Leadership For Learning: How to Help Teachers Succeed provides useful insights into some of the reasons for marginal teacher performance. According to its author, Carl Glickman, a teacher's inability to think abstractly and lack of motivation or commitment are the primary sources of poor teaching behavior. The following sections address these problems.

Abstract Thinking and Problem-Solving in the Classroom

Effective problem solving is essential to good teaching. In the course of a single class, a teacher is confronted with many problems that require immediate solutions. Capable teachers are able to generate solutions and act on them. A teacher in need of assistance who has difficulty thinking abstractly may not recognize a problem when it occurs, and if the problem is highlighted for him, he may not understand how to solve it. It may be hard for him to imagine making changes, and he may be unaware of the relationship between his actions in the classroom and the success of his students. When his students fail to learn, he may believe that they are at fault.

Glickman describes a teacher with these characteristics as having a low level of abstraction. A high abstractor, on the other hand, typically can diagnose problems and generate solutions. He understands the relationship between his actions and his students' success. He takes responsibility for instruction and its impact on students.

If a teacher is performing poorly because of a low level of abstraction, the supervisor or consulting teacher should first strive to understand the cause of the problem. Below are five possible causes of low abstraction and some strategies for supervision.

Lack of Experience

Beginning teachers in particular often expend all of their physical and emotional energy just to get through each lesson. Each lesson is planned and taught for the first time – a frustration that veteran educators may well have forgotten! While a new teacher may be aware of instructional or management problems, he lacks sufficient experience from which to draw possible solutions. At other times he may not even be aware that problems exist; to him, everything is operating just as it should. Recognizing the need to provide beginning teachers with additional support, California implemented the BTSA in 1997, and many districts have developed effective induction programs for beginning teachers.

Lack of Knowledge

For this discussion, we'll assume that the teacher is knowledgeable about the subject he is teaching. Chapter 7 addresses supervisory and documentation strategies to use when he is not.

Most teachers plan their daily lessons within an instructional comfort zone that is defined by what they know how to do and what they are comfortable doing, and they may not teach well because they simply do not know or understand instructional strategies that lie beyond their current practices. This lack of knowledge may increase when teachers are faced with students from different cultural, social, ethnic and/or economic backgrounds than students they have taught in the past. While effective in one teaching context, past teaching practices may not work with the current student group. Rather than admit that their reliance on traditional teaching practices is at fault, these teachers may blame students for their ineffectiveness.

Many teachers respond predictably to problems that arise in the classroom. For example, a beginning teacher may have a limited repertoire of skills for classroom management or for delivery of instruction. A more experienced teacher who finds the students in his classroom culturally, economically or ethnically different from those he is used to teaching may become frustrated when the strategies he considers "tried-and-true" no longer work. The teacher in need of assistance is often a teacher who has failed to learn and/or implement new instructional strategies, as in the case of the ten-year veteran who has had the same year of teaching experience ten times. This teacher may face mounting classroom problems when his limited teaching practices prove ineffective.

Difficulty Solving Problems

Sometimes a teacher in need of assistance recognizes the problems in his classroom but does not understand how to solve them. Even when problems and solutions are identified, he may adopt a "just show me what you want me to do" attitude rather than taking the initiative to transform possible solutions into concrete action.

Lack of Awareness

An effective teacher with a high level of abstraction is able to analyze instructional decisions that are made before and during a lesson and routinely questions his instructional choices: Why did I choose this demonstration technique? Why did I use these materials? Were my materials effective? Could I have used better examples? What strategies did I plan to make certain that students were actively participating in the learning process? He makes conscious decisions both in planning the lesson and in implementing moment-to-moment adjustments during instruction, and he reflects upon the thought processes that guide his instructional practices.

On the other hand, the teacher who is in need of assistance because of a low level of abstraction may be operating more from habit or from intuition than from conscious decision-making, and he may fail to see the connection between what he does and what his students do. He may be unaware that few students are participating, that many students are not understanding the instruction, or that several students have disengaged from the lesson. Teachers with low levels of abstraction may fail to recognize that the true measure of good teaching is the level of student engagement and success it evokes. As one teacher told co-author John Crain, "I think you should really observe me teach without any students in the room. Then you could see what my teaching is really like." This is a truly low abstractor!

Personal Problems

A teacher experiencing a serious crisis in his life outside the classroom may find himself emotionally and psychologically drained. If his problems diminish his classroom performance, his students may suffer. Marital difficulties or problems with family members, illness or injury, and financial woes may so occupy his attention that he is unable to devote much time and energy to the task of teaching, leaving him little to give once he arrives at school.

The supervisor or consulting teacher must be sensitive to the teacher's problems while remaining attentive to the needs of his students. If his problems persist, it may become necessary to consider whether his problems are impairing his classroom effectiveness and whether the problems are remediable.

Level of Commitment

Suppose one of the teachers you supervise or mentor can think abstractly and has no difficulty solving classroom problems, and yet she is still only marginally effective. In this case, you will need to consider her general attitude toward the teaching profession and toward her specific instructional responsibilities – in other words, how high is her level of commitment.

A low level of commitment may be caused by a deliberate "why bother" decision, or it may be a result of circumstances beyond the teacher's immediate control.

A teacher whose level of commitment is low may see no need to change, claiming that everything is "just fine." On the other hand, she may be the teacher who talks positively about changes but fails to follow through with effective action. Another manifestation of low commitment is the egocentric "what's in it for me?" attitude. The self-centered teacher fails to take action or make changes unless she can see some benefit for herself. Contrast this type of teacher with the highly motivated and committed teacher who is concerned about her students, her school, and the profession in general; who sees problems, chooses among alternative solutions, and follows through with decisions; or who continually seeks improvement and strives to make teaching and learning more interesting and exciting.

In the preceding section, we noted that supervision of the teacher in need of assistance because of a low level of abstraction requires assistance that extends beyond identifying classroom problems and their symptoms. The same is true when you supervise a teacher who lacks commitment. In order to make informed decisions regarding remediation, the supervisor or mentor must identify and address the causes of low levels of commitment. As with the abstraction issue, the following is not an exhaustive list of causes, but it does provide a beginning point for supervision.

Burnout

The education literature is full of reports about teacher burnout. Some teachers have become frustrated because students today are very different from students they taught in the past. These teachers are often less effective in working with increasingly diverse student populations. While once quite effective, these teachers may simply have stopped trying. Others are disillusioned by what they perceive as administrative and bureaucratic structures that limit or interfere with their classroom autonomy. In addition, misunderstandings and misinterpretations of the district's teacher evaluation system or the Standardized Testing and Reporting (STAR) Program may contribute to teacher frustration and burnout.

Self-Centeredness

Beginning teachers, in particular, may lack sufficient commitment because they are struggling to establish themselves professionally and to balance the demands of their personal and professional lives. It is difficult to make a commitment to be innovative and creative when just attending to the basics is overwhelming.

An experienced but ineffective teacher may be quite satisfied with the status quo and see little reason to change. Perhaps the teacher has good ideas but is unwilling to commit the necessary time and energy to carry them out. Her "What's in it for me? Why should I work harder and change what I do?" attitude suggests that she is more concerned with her own interests than with the needs of her students.

Unwillingness to Change and Fear of Change

Closely related to self-centeredness is the issue of change. Some teachers may simply be unwilling to change. They may realize that their old ways of teaching are not effective, but they are unwilling to commit the time and energy needed to learn and apply new pedagogy. Change sometimes involves learning about and acting on new insights into the teaching-and-learning process: learning styles, brain research, inductive/inquiry lessons, and learning characteristics of children living in a culture of generational poverty. Some teachers may want society and students to change so that the old ways of doing business in the classroom can be perpetuated. They complain that poor parenting and social problems are the cause of low student achievement and resist pressure to adapt their teaching practices to include methods that are more effective for contemporary student populations. Other teachers may simply fear change. Changing approaches to the design and delivery of instruction requires more risk than many are willing to accept, and there is comfort and safety in the old ways of doing things.

Personal Problems

While personal problems may hinder a teacher's ability to think abstractly and solve classroom problems, as discussed previously, they also may interfere with her commitment to her duties. The same marital or family difficulties, health problems, or financial stresses may occupy so much attention and energy that she is unable to devote significant time and energy to her professional obligations. It is difficult for the teacher to be highly motivated and committed to the job when her attention is absorbed by personal issues.

THE ISSUES INVOLVED IN SUPERVISION

In instructional supervision, there are four issues that the supervisor needs to consider: diagnosis, prescription, standards, and time lines.

Diagnosis

In diagnosing instructional problems, the supervisor, peer coach, or consulting teacher observes classroom instruction and/or examines a portfolio of student work and then draws conclusions about whether or not instructional practices meet standards. The diagnosis may address issues related to the level of student success, depth and complexity of the learning, connectivity of the learning to other disciplines and/or the world beyond the classroom, and the degree to which the classroom environment was effective for student learning.

Prescription

Depending on the diagnosis, the prescription sets a general direction for improved teaching behavior. Effective teachers may need no prescription, but struggling teachers will need help in identifying areas for change and the direction in which changes must take place.

Standards in Terms of Specific Teacher and Student Behaviors

While the prescription establishes a general direction for change, specifying standards for improvement clarifies the extent to which changes are required. Explaining the standard of instructional behavior that is required is essential to assisting teachers improve and assessing whether improvement takes place. The following examples illustrate the movement from general prescription to specific standard:

GENERAL PRESCRIPTION	SPECIFIC STANDARD
There will be more active participation in the teaching/learning process.	The teacher will utilize random questioning so that the majority of students are actively participating in the teaching/learning process.
There must be a more orderly classroom.	The teacher will monitor all students and stop or redirect behavior that is inappropriate or disruptive.

Time Lines

Time lines establish checkpoints at which teaching behaviors are expected to change and/or at which professional growth activities must be completed. When considering improvements in instructional behaviors, a common question is, "How much time is reasonable for improvement to occur?" The answer may be somewhat ambiguous because the length of time that is reasonable depends on a number of variables, including the teacher's status, length of service, previous evaluations, and the complexity of the needed changes in the teacher's behavior, as well as district policies and collective bargaining agreements.

Longer Time To Improve		**Shorter Time To Improve**
• Permanent Status	vs.	Probationary Status
• Multiple years of experience	vs.	New to teaching
• History of good evaluations	vs.	No evaluations or consistently weak evaluations
• Complex changes in teacher behavior	vs.	Simple changes in teacher behavior

When the desired changes in behavior are complex (e.g., designing student-centered, inductive/inquiry lessons instead of teacher-centered, deductive lessons), it is reasonable to expect an extended period of time for those changes to occur. However, if the desired changes in behavior are rather simple (e.g., post rules for student behavior in the classroom), it is reasonable to expect changes within a much shorter time frame.

There may be some behaviors that are not remediable and will require no time for improvement. Assaulting a student would probably be considered irremediable behavior.

MATCHING SUPERVISORY STYLE WITH TEACHER LEVEL OF DEVELOPMENT

Who Controls These Four Issues?

Supervisory goals are generally focused on assisting teachers in improving their instructional practices and professional habit, and a central concern of administrators is how to match their supervisory style to individual needs of the teachers they support. In this handbook we consider three supervisory styles: collaborative, nondirective and directive. Each of these styles requires a different level of supervisory control. (We address the appropriate styles for peer coaches and consulting teachers later in this chapter.) When the collaborative style is employed, the supervisor and teacher share control of diagnosis, prescription, standards and time lines. A nondirective approach places the teacher in control of her improvement. And a supervisor implementing the directive supervisory style retains control over all supervisory issues. Each of these supervisory styles supports improved instructional practice when properly implemented and appropriately applied.

The modified version of Carl Glickman's paradigm shown in the figure below and the discussion which follows suggest ways that you may achieve this match by using what you know about the teacher's level of abstraction and level of commitment. (**Note:** While the paradigm is Professor Glickman's, the interpretations and applications are those of the authors.)

Figure 3-1

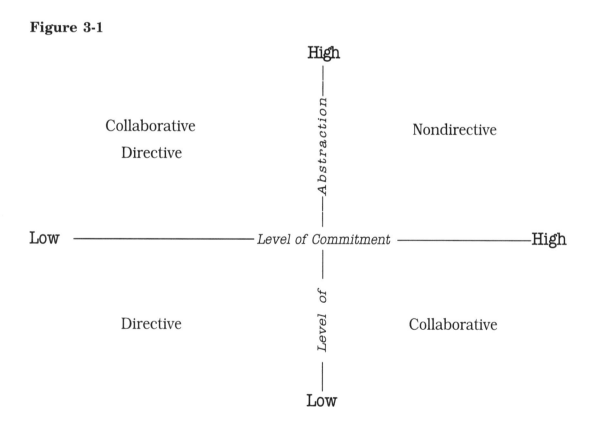

Since we are focusing on the teacher in need of assistance, we concentrate our examples of appropriate supervision styles for teachers in Quadrants I through III. The Quadrant IV teacher is, in general, the effective teacher.

Quadrant I

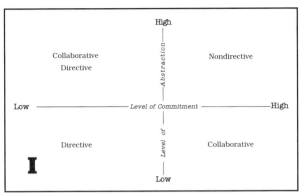

Abstraction Level: Low

Commitment Level: Low

A directive style probably is most appropriate for the Quadrant I teacher. Remember, this teacher has a low level of abstraction and a low level of commitment. Consider the following scenario:

> In the post-observation conference, you tell the teacher that you observed four students passing notes. Then she responds, "Which students? When were they passing notes?" Later in the conference, you tell her that during the 45 minutes of observation three of the 28 students participated in the lesson in ways other than passive listening and note-taking. The teacher responds, "Is that a problem?" Toward the end of the conference, you ask her what changes she would make if she were to teach the same lesson again tomorrow. She replies: "I'd probably do it pretty much the same way. These remedial-level kids aren't going to do anything no matter what I do."

This teacher needs a directive style of supervision if any changes are going to occur. Her inability to see the problems in her classroom demonstrates her low level of abstraction, and even when problems are identified, she does not understand how to solve them. The directive supervisory style will be the most effective approach in this situation, and the supervisor must control the issues of diagnosis and prescription.

In addition, the post-observation conference revealed that this teacher thinks the students are the problem and that not much change will take place as a result of her initiative. Clearly, her level of commitment is low; therefore, you also must control the standards and time lines for her improvement.

> **QUADRANT I**
> Directive Supervision
> *Supervisor Controls*
> - Diagnosis
> - Prescription
> - Standards
> - Time Lines

The Quadrant I teacher is unlikely to improve unless you use a directive supervisory style, and if your goal is contract nonextension or termination, the directive approach is required.

Quadrant II

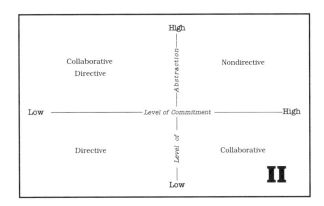

Abstraction Level: Low

Commitment Level: High

A collaborative style is most appropriate for the Quadrant II teacher. Recall from our previous discussion that many beginning teachers are in this quadrant. The following scenario illustrates how to work with a teacher who has a high level of commitment but whose low level of abstraction hinders his effectiveness.

In the post-observation conference, you share with the teacher some of the data you gathered during the observation. You tell him that when students were successful in responding to questions, he simply called on the next student and that when students were unsuccessful he provided no prompting or corrective feedback. The teacher is surprised. "I really thought I was using more positive reinforcement with the kids. I really enjoy them, and I want them to feel good when they are successful. I know I'm not very good at giving corrective feedback and prompting. I'm always so afraid I'll make them feel dumb or embarrass them if I try to help them get the right answer." When he asks you what he can do to improve both situations, you offer a number of alternatives. He replies, "I'd really like to attend the workshop on instructional strategies for low-achieving students and to observe Mr. Jones. He's really good at helping his kids without making them feel bad." He then asks if you can come back to observe immediately after he attends the workshop and observes Mr. Jones to see if he has improved. You suggest that maybe two weeks after the workshop and the observation of Mr. Jones' class would be a better time for you to revisit his classroom. This will give the teacher time to practice what he has learned.

QUADRANT II
Collaborative Supervision
Supervisor and Teacher
Share Control
- Diagnosis
- Prescription
- Standards
- Time Lines

This teacher is aware of some problems but not of others. In discussing the problems, he indicates that he is not quite sure how to solve them. If the goal is to help the teacher improve, you need to share control of the diagnosis and prescription by presenting the objective data from the observation and offering a range of suggestions from which the teacher may choose. Fortunately, this teacher has a high level of commitment. He wants to be better at both positive reinforcement and corrective feedback and even suggests one strategy for improvement. He asks you to return to the classroom to see if he has improved. You share control of the standards and time lines, not because the teacher lacks commitment, but because he is inclined to overcommit to both the complexity and the speed of change.

You may find yourself supervising a Quadrant II teacher who wants to improve and who has a high level of commitment but whose level of abstraction is so low that improvement within a reasonable period of time is unlikely. In this instance, you may want to consider shifting your supervisory style from collaborative to directive.

Quadrant III

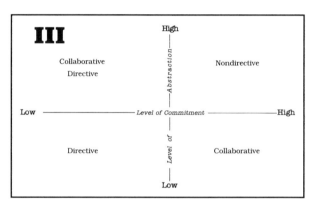

Abstraction Level: High

Commitment Level: Low

If your goal is to help the Quadrant III teacher improve, a collaborative style may be effective for diagnosis and prescription; on standards and time lines, a directive style probably will be most appropriate.

In the post-observation conference, you tell the teacher that when you were observing her lesson, she put the term "existentialism" on the board and proceeded to talk about Jean-Paul Sartre and how he influenced a whole generation of American writers. When students were asked what Sartre's influence was on three short stories they recently had read, none of the six students called on was able to give a correct answer. When she assigned a three-paragraph in-class essay on Sartre's influence on the stories, at least nine students just sat at their desks looking at blank paper. At least six others had their hands up constantly. The teacher replied, "I know they had no idea what to do. I probably should have identified the four or five characteristics of existentialism and given them some examples before asking questions and making the writing assignment. I know from Madeline Hunter's work that abstract concepts are made more understandable and concrete for students if the critical attributes can be identified and elaborated. I will certainly need to do that in the future." Two weeks later, you observe the teacher teaching a lesson on Romanticism in American literature. She teaches this lesson in exactly the same way as she taught the lesson on existentialism and with the same effect on students.

QUADRANT III

Collaborative Supervision for Diagnosis and Prescription
Teacher and Supervisor May Share Control

- Diagnosis
- Prescription

· · · · · · · · · · · · · · · · · · ·

Direct Supervision for Standards and Time Lines
Supervisor Controls

- Standards
- Time Lines

This teacher has a high level of abstraction. She knows the problem, how to address the problem, what the options are, and the research literature. She has the ability to share control of diagnosis and prescription issues with the supervisor. In this instance she does so accurately. However, this teacher's lack of commitment becomes apparent when her teaching style remains the same even after the need for change was discussed in the post-observation conference. The supervisor, therefore, needs to control the standards and time lines by telling this teacher what to do and setting a definite deadline for doing it.

Quadrant IV

Abstraction Level: High

Commitment Level: High

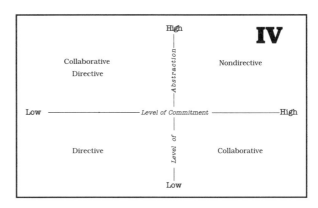

It is unlikely that you will ever need to use a directive approach with a Quadrant IV teacher. It is equally unlikely that a peer coach or consulting teacher would ever be assigned to work with a Quadrant IV teacher. This teacher has a high level of abstraction and a high level of commitment. If you are a PAR consulting teacher, you are probably a Quadrant IV teacher! Consider the following scenario:

In the post-observation conference, you ask the teacher to reflect on the mathematics lesson you observed. The teacher tells you that he is generally pleased with the way the lesson went. "The students were all engaged and almost all of them participated when I was demonstrating the algorithm on the overhead. I know that's sometimes hard for them to do." When you ask the teacher why he believes the level of engagement and participation were so high, he says, "Well, I think there are several reasons. I try to apply the concepts we study to things that are relevant to them. In this lesson, I used data from the entertainment industry in southern California-especially the trend data from the music industry. There's usually more motivation to be engaged when the mathematical questions are interesting and relevant." You ask the teacher what he would want to do differently in future lessons. The teacher replies, "I really want to move away from so much traditional paper/pencil assessment of their learning. I've been reading about problem-based learning in the math journals. That approach calls on students to produce products or performances that demonstrate that they understand and can apply the math. I'd really like to learn more about that and begin to try it out—maybe some time next semester."

A nondirective style clearly will be most appropriate because his high levels of abstraction and commitment make him effective. He recognizes what works in his class and can articulate the strategies he implements. He reads the literature in his field and is familiar with other options available to him. He is quite capable of controlling his own diagnosis and prescription. Since it reasonably can be anticipated that this teacher will take action to repeat effective behaviors and work to improve ineffective behaviors, the supervisor also should allow him to control standards and time lines.

QUADRANT IV
Nondirective Supervision
Teacher Controls
- Diagnosis
- Prescription
- Standards
- Time Lines

STRATEGIES FOR COLLABORATION

As indicated above, the collaborative supervisory style is often appropriate in cases involving teachers in need of assistance (Quadrant II, in particular). This approach is particularly useful for the peer coach or PAR consulting teacher, who lacks supervisory authority. The steps listed below are part of an overall strategy of collaborative supervision. Their use, of course, will be determined by district policies and procedures and collective bargaining contract provisions.

1. Conduct pre-observation conferences to discuss the teacher's plans for the lesson and what you will expect to see (e.g., instructional strategies, classroom management practices, techniques of presentation of subject matter, learning climate, evidence of successful student performance).

2. Conduct classroom observations, collect data, analyze the data, and make your own preliminary determination about the practices that are effective in terms of successful student behavior/performance and those that are not.

3. After each observation, conduct a post-observation conference. In the conference, provide feedback on the issues discussed in the pre-observation conference and/or ask questions that encourage the teacher to analyze the lesson and the data. Remember that this is a collaborative conference, so you will be sharing control of the issues: diagnosis, prescription, standards, and time lines.

4. Diagnosis: This is a shared decision. Ask the teacher what she believes was or was not effective. Ask questions and provide data from the observation that prompt the teacher to identify teaching practices or lesson design that were or were not effective.

5. Prescription/Standards: This is a shared decision. Ask the teacher about what changes in teaching practices or lesson design should occur. Offer suggestions for alternative strategies and suggest professional development activities to help the teacher to bring about the changes.

6. Time lines: This is a shared decision. Set reasonable time frames for changes in behavior and for completion of professional growth activities in consultation with the teacher.

7. Write a focused observation memorandum following each conference. (See Chapters 5 through 9).

8. Continue to observe the teacher in the classroom, focusing on the specific changes in behavior that you and the teacher agreed to, as well gathering evidence of successful student performance. (See Chapters 5 through 9).

9. If necessary, write a professional growth plan to formalize your judgments regarding deficiencies (diagnosis), your directives for changes in a classroom behavior (prescription and standards), your expectations for student performance, and time lines for successful implementation of the standards. (See Chapter 4).

STRATEGIES FOR DIRECT SUPERVISION

As indicated above, the directive supervisory style is often appropriate for cases involving marginally effective or ineffective teachers and is most appropriately used by school administrators. The steps listed below are part of an overall strategy of directive supervision.

1. Conduct pre-observation conferences to discuss the teacher's plans for the lesson and what you will expect to see (e.g., instructional strategies, classroom management practices, techniques of presentation of subject matter, learning climate, evidence of successful student performance).

2. Conduct frequent classroom observations, collect data, and analyze the data to determine which practices are effective and which are not in terms of successful student behavior/performance.

3. After each observation, conduct a post-observation conference to provide feedback on the issues discussed in the pre-observation conference. Remember that this is a directive conference, so you will be in control (not shared control) of the issues: diagnosis, prescription, standards, and time lines.

4. Diagnosis: You have control of this issue. Be very specific about what was or was not effective.

5. Prescription/standards: You have control of this issue. Be very specific about what additional changes must occur. Suggest or require professional development activities to help bring about the needed changes.

6. Time lines: You have control of this issue. Set reasonable time frames for changes in behavior and for completion of professional growth activities.

7. Write a focused observation memorandum following each conference. (See Chapters 5 through 9).

8. Continue to observe the teacher in the classroom, focusing on the specific changes in behavior that you directed and on evidence of successful student performance. (See Chapters 5 through 9).

9. Write a professional growth plan to formalize your judgments regarding deficiencies (diagnosis), your directives for changes in a classroom behavior (prescription and standards), your expectations for student performance, and time lines for successful implementation of the standards. (See Chapter 4).

Note: The teacher's failure to follow directives to change instructional behavior may become be the basis for decisions to nonextend or terminate the teaching contract.

A NOTE TO PEER COACHES AND CONSULTING TEACHERS

If you are a consulting teacher or peer coach, your position is one of mentorship and it is your responsibility to act as a coach, providing support and assistance to struggling teachers. As such, it is probably not appropriate for you to formally evaluate or issue directives to the teacher or teachers with whom you work. Thus the directive style of supervision will be of little use to you. You will recall that the directive approach is generally reserved for Quadrant I and III teachers and requires that supervisors control the diagnosis, prescription, standards and timelines for improvement. Clearly this approach is best employed by persons vested with the authority to make personnel decisions.

It is equally unlikely that you will rely exclusively on the nondirective mode in your role as a consulting teacher. Recall that the nondirective approach is reserved for Quadrant IV teachers who generally have a high level of abstraction and commitment. Quadrant IV teachers are often recognized as "master teachers" and it is improbable that such a teacher will be referred for PAR assistance or require peer coaching.

Instead, your style of interaction is most likely to be a combination of collaborative and nondirective, the styles in which you and the teacher share control of the supervision issues: diagnosis, prescription, standards, and time lines. Let's take a moment to examine the implications of these approaches for consulting teachers.

Diagnosis and Prescription

You will recall that diagnosis is the identification of effective and ineffective teaching behaviors and that prescription consists of focusing the teacher on the general direction in which change or improvement should take place. Prescriptive advice may be couched in terms of either teacher or student behaviors. For example: The teacher must actively monitor students during seat work. Or: Students should spend more time engaged in on-task activities.

Remember that many teachers referred to PAR may have low levels of abstraction. That is, they may not fully recognize when problems exist, and they may not understand how to solve these problems once they have been identified. It is your job to focus the teacher on the problems and guide him or her toward solutions through careful questioning and coaching, and by offering suggestions and insights rooted in your own teaching experiences.

In the post-observation conference, it is probably best to begin your discussion with open-ended diagnostic questions, such as "What do you think was successful in this lesson?" and "If you could teach this lesson again, is there anything you would do differently?" If the teacher's responses demonstrate that she has reflected on the lesson and if her insights are appropriate, you can reinforce her diagnosis and begin a discussion of prescriptive possibilities. In maintaining a nondirective and collaborative approach (shared control), you should allow the teacher to suggest possible remedies and your discussion should guide the teacher toward appropriate strategies that she may have not considered. You may choose to ask questions framed in language such as:

- "Have you ever tried . . . ?"
- "Have you ever considered . . . ?"
- "What would you think about . . . ?" or
- "What do you think would happen if you . . . ?"

If the teacher is unable or unwilling to provide an effective diagnosis of the lesson, the post-observation conference will need to be one of data sharing. This task will be made much easier if you have completed one of the focused observation instruments presented in the following chapters. It is probably best to begin the discussion with positive observations, no matter how few or how trivial they may be, and then move to the items that indicate the lesson was poorly taught. As a consulting teacher, it is important that you maintain an objective, non-critical tone and a positive attitude in relating what you have observed. For example, your summary of the observation data might allow you to share the following information:

> While the students were working in their groups, I walked around to observe them and to examine what they were doing. Of the six learning groups, two were not working on the task that you assigned and two other groups were having some difficulty with the assignment. You worked with one group for the full 30 minutes of the activity.

In sharing this objective data non-critically, you provide the teacher with an opportunity to reflect on and respond to your observations. When the teacher is prompted in such a manner, she is very likely to recognize the problem, and you can smoothly transition to a discussion of what could have been done differently. If she is unable (or unwilling) to recognize the problem, you will have to take more control of the diagnosis and prescription by telling her what the data are suggesting. For example, you might say:

> The first standard of the California Standards for the Teaching Profession and our local district evaluation standards require teachers to "engage and support all students in learning." In terms of student behavior, this means that most students actively and successfully participate in the lesson. The data from my observation suggest that this standard is not being met. What do you think you could do differently in order to meet this standard in the future?

Standards and Time Lines

You will recall that standards are the specific classroom behaviors that should change and time lines address when changes in behavior will occur. Since you are using a nondirective and collaborative mode, you and the teacher will share control of these issues. In discussing standards, it may be useful to consider the reasons the teacher was referred for PAR intervention or peer coaching and to identify the criteria for improvement established by the PAR committee and the teacher's supervisor. These criteria frame the expectations for behavioral change. As a peer coach or consulting teacher, your job is to coach the teacher to an acceptable level of performance. In collaborating with the teacher, you will work to identify paths to improvement and help the teacher to recognize what improvement means in terms of both teacher and student behaviors. The open-ended questioning strategy will be useful in suggesting techniques that will lead to improvement while allowing the teacher to decide which techniques to implement. Consider framing your suggestions in the following manner:

- "Would you be willing to consider . . . ?"
- "What would you think about . . . ?"
- "Are you aware of . . . ?"
- "Would you consider trying . . . ?"

This style of questioning allows you to control much of the discussion, but allows the teacher decision making control over which strategies to implement.

When discussing time lines, encourage the teacher to be reasonable about his expectations for change. Changes in more complex teacher behaviors will require more time to improve. For example, moving from teacher-centered to student-centered instruction or implementing inductive/inquiry lessons are complex tasks and will require more time for improvement. Posting classroom rules, devising a system for handing out or taking up materials, and using students names are simpler changes and will require less time. In some instances, you may need to counsel patience. A teacher who is eager to improve may have unrealistic expectations of the amount of time and effort the improvements will require. In other cases, you may need to prompt reluctant teachers to implement changes in a more timely fashion

Consulting teachers and peer coaches may find it challenging to remain in a collaborative mode with teachers who lack the experience or insight to recognize ineffective teaching behaviors and the strategies for improvement. It is very easy to slip into the directive style and to simply tell the struggling teacher what to do. This is of limited use however, because your goal is to make the teacher more self-directed and reflective with respect to his teaching behaviors. To achieve this end you must act as counselor, coach and confidant. The teacher or teachers you mentor must be able to rely on your non-critical approach to what you observe in their classrooms and to what they share in discussions about their teaching. A sense of humor will be a great asset in achieving this goal and will ease the tension for teachers who may feel discouraged, embarassed, or insulted by their inclusion in the PAR intervention or peer coaching process. Above all, remember that peer coaches and consulting teachers perform a very important service to both the teaching profession and to students. It is no small task to assist a struggling teacher to improve, but when improvement takes place the entire school community benefits.

DEALING WITH CLAIMS OF HARASSMENT

It should be clear from our discussion so far that the supervisor responsible for teachers in need of assistance will be spending considerable time in their classrooms. A teacher who resents your increased attention may accuse you of harassment, claiming that she is the subject of "arbitrary and capricious treatment." Why else would you be spending so much time in her classroom in comparison with the time spent in the classrooms of other teachers? Claims of harassment are unlikely to be given much credence when the rationale for stepped-up classroom visitations is objectively clear. There are a number of tactics you can use to forestall allegations of harassment and arbitrary and capricious treatment. Begin by making certain that you do, in fact, have objective reasons for visiting the teacher's classroom more frequently. The following list includes sample reasons for spending more time in a classroom. Whether they apply in a given school will depend on your district's policy and the collective bargaining agreement.

• Deficiencies have been apparent in previous classroom observations.

• Monitoring the requirements of a remediation plan.

• Failure rates that exceed the norm for your campus.

- Complaints from parents, students, or other staff members.

- Low student performance indicated by the results of STAR tests.

- Uniform treatment of an entire "class" of teachers (e.g., all probationary contract teachers, all teachers in their first year of assignment to your campus); if your campus plan has targeted raising math scores, the "class" of teacher may be all math teachers.

Explain to the teacher in need of assistance that your purpose is to help, not hurt. Comments such as these might be useful:

> "As you know, Ms. Jones, my formal observations have revealed some significant deficiencies in your classroom performance. I am going to devote as much of my time as possible to helping you improve. I will be visiting your classes periodically to see how our professional growth plan is working and to learn what else we might do. Please don't be upset by my visits. My purpose is to help you overcome these problems so that you can realize your full potential as a teacher on this campus."

It is true, of course, that you may eventually conclude that Ms. Jones will never be an effective teacher. Because of low abstraction and/or commitment levels, some marginally effective teachers cannot and/or will not respond favorably to guidance and principles of good developmental supervision. In these instances, it may become necessary for you as the supervisor to recommend contract nonextension or, in the case of the permanent teacher, contract termination.

SUMMARY

In this chapter we have addressed the sources of poor instructional behaviors – low levels abstraction and commitment – and discussed the supervisory issues and approaches that affect and support instructional improvement and professional growth in teachers in need of assistance. In addition, we have discussed how peer coaches and PAR consulting teachers can best adapt these approaches to the demands of mentoring and coaching improvement in struggling teachers. In Chapter 4 we will address the development of professional growth plans that clearly communicate directives for change, and in the following chapters we will discuss classroom observation and documentation techniques designed to facilitate better instructional behaviors and improved student outcomes.

CHAPTER FOUR: WRITING AND MONITORING PROFESSIONAL GROWTH PLANS

While the California Education Code does not require school districts to develop and implement professional growth plans (PGPs) addressing classroom instruction for probationary or permanent contract teachers, many districts find that the use of growth plans facilitates professional development, improves classroom instruction and positively affects student achievement. In addition, carefully developed PGPs may help districts meet Peer Assistance and Review (PAR) requirements.

Section 44500 of the Education Code outlines PAR's requirements. While considerable discretion is left to districts with respect to the structure of individual PAR programs, the implementing legislation requires:

- Clearly written performance goals, aligned with student learning, and consistent with academic content standards (§ 44500 (b)(2));

- Multiple classroom observations of teachers participating in the PAR process (§ 44500 (b)(3));

- Staff development activities designed to assist teachers improve instructional skills and knowledge teaching skills (§ 44500 (b)(5));

- A monitoring component with a written record (§ 44500 (b)(6)).

To our way of thinking, the development of professional growth plans is an excellent way to comply with these provisions. A PGP will help in the remediation and support of teachers referred for PAR intervention and will provide important documentation in the event that contract nonextension (probationary teacher) or termination (permanent teacher) is recommended.

As discussed in the first chapter of this handbook, the law presents a number of reasons for negative employment decisions. In the case of teachers with poor instructional habits and ineffective classroom practices, the strongest evidence and most objective rationale supporting dismissal are rooted in a teacher's failure to meet state and district instructional standards and lack of compliance with administrative directives for improvement. Administrative directives addressing instructional issues can be communicated effectively through a PGP. And in the case of contract nonextension or termination, demonstrating that a teacher has failed to comply with the requirements of a growth plan is easier and much less inflammatory than proving that the teacher is incompetent.

HOW TO WRITE A PROFESSIONAL GROWTH PLAN

A well-written PGP consists of the following four components, each of which is explained in this chapter:

1. Notice that improvement or change is needed;

2. Specific directives for improvement, including those linked to student performance;

3. Offers of assistance and support; and

4. Reasonable time lines for the achievement of growth and improvement.

Notification that Improvement or Change is Needed

It is the ethical and legal responsibility of supervisors to alert teachers to conduct or classroom performance that does not meet district expectations. In directing improvement or change, supervisors may need to address issues or problems with both in- and out-of-class behaviors.

Problems Outside the Classroom

You may recall from Chapters 1 and 2 that Ima Leader had experienced difficulties with Bob Instructor's attendance practices. Attendance problems are a common area of professional weakness that do not involve in-class behaviors directly. Some other areas include failure to complete written lesson plans, failure to adhere to district and campus policies and procedures, ignoring assignments for campus supervision, failure to report grades in a timely manner, and inappropriate conduct during staff meetings. If a teacher is deficient in one of these areas, a clearly worded statement that directs change or improvement is needed:

1. You must follow district/campus policies in reporting student grades to the office and to parents.

2. You must write lesson plans according to the campus format and submit them to the principal's office.

3. You must be present at your assigned duty station fifteen minutes before and fifteen minutes after school.

Instruction and Classroom Management Problems

Effective documentation of instruction is essential to establishing that observed classroom behaviors do not meet district expectations. Data collected during classroom observations will help to determine whether teachers are meeting state and local teaching standards and will highlight the changes that supervisors will need to direct. For example, a teacher who demonstrates poor performance with respect to the first CSTP standard, Engaging and Supporting All Students in Learning, might receive the following directives in his PGP:

Your current instructional practices with respect to the first standard of the California Standards for the Teaching Profession, Engaging and Supporting All Students in Learning, do not meet standards. The following elements of the standard need improvement:

1. Making connections between students' prior knowledge, their interests and experiences and the content of current instruction;

2. Providing opportunities for students to engage in critical thinking and problem solving activities; and

3. Providing activities in which students have opportunities for self-directed learning.

Note that these statements are somewhat broadly worded, much like the "prescriptions" that were discussed in Chapter 3. The next section of the growth plan will set out specific directives for improvement and change.

Giving Specific Directives for Improvement

Directives for Professional Growth Activities

Most directives related to professional improvement *activities* are simply constructed statements that include such things as:

- Each Monday submit a lesson plan that incorporates problem solving, critical thinking skills, and other application level activities into the sequence of instruction.

- Observe another teacher no later than the end of September and schedule a conference with the principal to discuss the observation.

- Attend a designated district training session on engaging students in activities that make subject matter more meaningful.

While directives related to activities are important components of a growth plan, if they are the only directives given, supervisors may encounter problems. Suppose the teacher who received the directives cited above provides documentation of his compliance. When the supervisor revisits his classroom, she observes him doing pretty much what he did before, with much the same result—lack of student engagement. Nothing has changed, and yet the teacher has complied with all administrative directives! The problem with directives for professional growth activities is that they generally do not include references to behavioral changes, so it is entirely possible for the teacher to complete all the directed activities without making any adjustments to his teaching behaviors. A teacher union representative will be quick to point out that the teacher has complied with all directives, and therefore has met the requirements of his growth plan.

Directives for Changes in Teacher Behavior

While the directives for professional growth activities given above are certainly valuable, they are incomplete because they do not indicate that *teacher behaviors* must change. The teacher's problem is not that he failed to submit lesson plans, observe other teachers, or attend workshops; instead, it is his behavior that is the source of his difficulties. Because the supervisor's primary goals are to help the teacher improve his instructional practices and to facilitate student learning, her directives should describe her expectations for changes in specific teaching behaviors as well as activities for professional growth. These directives will form the standard against which she will conduct future classroom observations and measure change.

In writing such directives effectively, supervisors will find it useful to phrase statements in terms of cause and effect. Below find a chart that presents a formula for phrasing such directives in clear and effective terms:

Figure 4-1

INSTRUCTIONAL INDICATOR   EXPECTED OUTCOME

**Teacher behaves -------------------- so that ----------- students behave
a certain way   a certain way.**

(Teacher Behavior)   +   (Linking Words) —>   (Student Behavior)

Examples:

Teacher solicits
student participation ---------- in such a way that --- more students than not
are participating and
most are successful.

Teacher redirects
inappropriate behavior ----------------- so that ----------- students stop engaging
in inappropriate behavior.

Because the effectiveness of changed teaching behaviors is best measured in terms of student learning, these directives define expected outcomes in terms of student behaviors.

Why Include Student Behavior in the Directives?

There are two clear advantages to including student behavior in administrative directives. First, the focus in California, as in virtually all states, is on improving student achievement. This is the purpose of the state-mandated curriculum content standards and the accompanying California Standardized Testing and Reporting (STAR) Program. As noted in California Education Code § 60602 (a), the primary purpose of the student assessment system is to "improve teaching and learning" in California public classrooms. Therefore, references to student behaviors ensure that directives help to move both teachers and students toward state-required levels of proficiency.

Second, directives that include student behaviors reduce the likelihood of "dog and pony shows" in future classroom visits. While a teacher may be able to change *his* behavior the moment a supervisor steps into classroom, it is unlikely that his *students'* behavior will evidence change unless the teacher's improved behavior has been a consistent factor in daily classroom instruction.

Supervisors should be aware that some instructional behaviors do not have a corresponding objectively observable student outcome. Examples include teacher behaviors related to classroom learning environment such as (1) relating the lesson to student interests or experiences, (2) praising or reinforcing student learning, and (3) exhibiting courtesy and respect. Likewise, instructional behaviors such as beginning the lesson with an appropriate introduction and relating content to prior or future learning may not have an immediate, observable effect on student behavior. When directing changes in these types of instructional behaviors, it is best not to frame expected outcomes in terms of student responses.

In succeeding chapters, we will discuss how to write memoranda that direct changes in specific teaching behaviors and how to link these changes to student performance when appropriate.

Authority for Directives

When issuing directives as part of a professional growth plan, it is important to cite the source of authority for the directive. This helps to avoid accusations that directives are the result of subjective opinions or arbitrary and capricious supervisory whims. When possible, precede directives with phrases that include such language as:

- The California Standards for the Teaching Profession (CSTP) have an expectation that you . . .
- The school district appraisal system has an expectation that you . . .
- Our campus plan has an expectation that you . . .
- The grade-level curriculum content standards require that you . . .
- District (campus) policy requires that you . . .
- Your job description requires you to . . .

Success of Students Over Time

When considering teacher effectiveness with respect to student performance, it is often necessary to consider changes that occur over a period of time. The portfolio approach to student learning is a method that many schools and districts have incorporated to measure student progress. This method requires that teachers maintain collections or portfolios of student work products over a designated instructional period. In assessing student growth and success in the subject area, evaluators examine these portfolios and ask:

- Do the products reflect learning that has depth and complexity?
- Do the student's products connect learning to other disciplines, the world of work, and/or issues in the world beyond the classroom?
- Do the student's products demonstrate competence in content knowledge, critical thinking, and problem solving?

The evaluator's assessment of the quality of work contained in student portfolios can assist in determining whether a professional growth plan is needed or whether the requirements of an existing plan are being met. The quality of student portfolio work may help supervisors to discern needed changes in teaching behavior, frame written directives in terms of student outcomes, and measure improvements in instructional practices.

Professional Growth Plans and Standardized Testing

Attention to standardized testing is growing nationwide. Politicians, the media, and educational researchers increasingly point to scores on standardized tests as indicators of school performance and effectiveness, and there are increasing calls to link both administrator and teacher assessments to the results of standardized tests.

As noted earlier, California's system of standardized tests is contained in the Standardized Testing and Reporting (STAR) Program. The STAR Program is composed of four component tests:

1. The California Standards Tests (CSTs) — criterion-referenced tests given to students in grades two through eleven. The CSTs are produced for California's public schools and are aligned with state-adopted grade level curricular standards;

2. The California Achievement Tests Survey (CAT/6) — norm-referenced achievement tests developed for the state of California;

3. The Spanish Assessment of Basic Education (SABE/2) — a norm-referenced achievement test in Spanish; and

4. The California Alternative Performance Assessment (CAPA) — a test developed for students with significant disabilities who are not able to take the CSTs or the CAT/6.

California also provides a criterion-referenced achievement test for students in the process of learning English, the California English Language Development Test (CELDT).

When preparing students for testing and assessing test results, administrators and teachers will be primarily concerned with the California Standards Tests because these tests comprise the primary means of assessing student achievement relative to the state's curricular standards. Given the increasing emphasis on test results, supervisors are well advised to be attentive to test preparation methods when performing classroom observations and developing professional growth plans. In addition, some supervisors may wish to consider test results when setting performance goals.

The California Education Code limits classroom preparation for standardized tests, stating "No . . . district superintendent of schools or principal or teacher of any elementary or secondary school shall carry on any program of specific preparation for the statewide pupil assessment program or a particular test therein" (§ 60611), and title 5 of the California Code of Regulations reads, "no program or materials shall be used by a school district or employee of a school district that are specifically formulated or intended to prepare pupils for the designated achievement test" (§ 854 (a)). Title 5 permits the use of publisher provided practice tests for the "limited purpose of familiarizing pupils with the use of scannable test booklets or answer sheets and the format of test items" (§ 854 (b)). With these restrictions in mind, supervisors should be aware of inappropriate test preparation methods when observing and evaluating teachers and when writing directives.

As a rule of thumb, the California Department of Education's Standards and Assessment Division advises educators to consider whether their method of preparing students would change substantially if the test were replaced with a test of different type or format. If their method of test preparation would remain the same, it is probably permissible. If not, the case is not so clear. A brief listing of appropriate and inappropriate test preparation techniques includes:

APPROPRIATE TEST PREPARATION	INAPPROPRIATE TEST PREPARATION
• Using publisher provided practice tests • Preparing students with test-taking strategies, including using time efficiently, understanding directions and marking answers • Using problem solving techniques such as guessing, estimating, and eliminating incorrect answers • Recognizing test formats such as multiple choice, true-false statements, and negative wording	• Using actual test items or identically formatted test items in drills or practices • Conducting a test preparation program specifically targeted to the STAR Program • Using alternate forms of the test or copies of the test from previous years • Focusing on one type of writing in anticipation of the test prompt (California Writing Standards Test: grades 4 and 7)

(Source: California Department of Education, Standards and Assessment Division)

Supervisors and consulting teachers will want to be certain that teachers adhere to these policies when they conduct their classroom observations. In addition, supervisors will want to be sure that they do not write impermissible directives that ask teachers to breach these requirements.

Some administrators may choose to include testing outcomes when writing growth plan requirements. We advise the following format when writing such directives:

Linking Instructional Behaviors to Testing Outcomes

INSRUCTIONAL INDICATOR   EXPECTED OUTCOME

Teacher Behavior   +   *Linking Language* —>   *Student Behavior / Performance*

Design and deliver instruction that is aligned with the California content standards for ninth grade science ------------ in such a way that ---------- the percentage of students meeting minimum expectations (e.g. passing) the ninth grade end-of-course California Standards Test in science increases.

(Any of the teaching behaviors listed in CSTP) --------- in such a way that ---------- the percentage of students demonstrating English proficiency on the California English Language Development Test increases.

A word of caution:

The use of standardized test results as a measure of teacher effectiveness has not been fully established. Until it has, we urge the following cautions:

1. Include directives related to student performance on standardized tests only as part of a set of directives that encompasses teachers' classroom behaviors. Incorporate teaching indicators included in the state-adopted CSTP and/ or your locally adopted appraisal system.

2. Be cautious about setting specific goals for increases in the passing rate (e.g., ". . . so that 80% of students meet the minimum expectations"). If teachers or their union representatives perceive the set percentages as unreasonable or unfair, conflict is inevitable. Establish levels of performance that are proportionate with what capable teachers are accomplishing with similarly situated students. Supervisors probably will find that framing expectations in general terms, as we have done in the examples above, is the most effective means for writing directives related to test scores. More generalized goals will work to motivate improved test performance and avoid conflict with teachers and their union advocates.

3. Finally, recall our recommendation that supervisors cite the authority for their directives when writing growth plans. With respect to test expectations, that authority may be expressed as:

   • The California Writing Standards Test for the fourth grade requires students to produce four types of writing: narratives, summaries, information reports, and responses to literature.

   • The California Department of Education and our own district policy prohibit the use of drills or review exercises that have formats identical to items on standardized tests.

   • The California Academic Content Standards and the California Standards Test for seventh grade mathematics require that students are able to construct and read drawings and models made to scale.

Offering Assistance and Support

An effective PGP will also include a list of requirements designed to assist the teacher in complying with the plan's directives for improvement. From an ethical and professional point of view, the focus of these requirements is to help the teacher to meet expectations for instructional effectiveness and improve student learning. From a legal perspective, these requirements demonstrate that the teacher has been given opportunities to improve and that supervisory support has been provided. Including a second set of administrative directives related to remediation in the growth plan provides a solid basis for a recommendation of contract nonextension (probationary teacher) or termination (permanent teacher) if the teacher fails to improve.

Depending on district policy and the collective bargaining agreement, supervisors may direct struggling teachers to attend training sessions, observe other teachers, submit written lesson plans, or read relevant journal articles. And, of course, the PAR process is a central element in providing remediation and support for teachers experiencing difficulties. All directives should focus on providing assistance in meeting the behavioral expectations outlined in the first section of the PGP. A more complete listing of activities is found in Appendix C.

Providing a Reasonable Time Line for Growth and Improvement

There is no clear rule about time lines for demonstrating improvement, although many directives will require that teachers complete activities such as attending a workshop or obtaining training by a specified date. In Chapter 3, we outlined some factors that influence the amount of time allotted for instructional improvements. We revisit these factors below:

Complexity of Change	Time lines for simple changes such as developing and submitting a discipline management plan may be short. Complex changes in behavior, such as implementing cooperative learning, will take longer.
Previous Evaluations	The existence of previous negative evaluations may shorten a time line. Likewise, the existence of previous positive evaluations may extend the time line for improvement.
Type of Contract	Probationary contract teachers require shorter time lines. Permanent contract teachers may require longer time lines, especially if their previous evaluations have been positive.
Remediability	If behavior is remediable (e.g., changing instructional or classroom management practices, following campus/district policy, following campus/district policy), a longer time line may be required. If behavior is irremediable (e.g., sexual harassment or striking a student), no time line for improvement is required.

Supervisors also need to remember to update directives for improvement if the teacher complies with earlier directives but still remains deficient in some areas.

A Sample Professional Growth Plan

Below find a sample PGP rooted in the four components we cited earlier: (1) notice that improvement or change is needed, (2) specific directives for improvement, (3) offers of assistance and support, and (4) provision of a reasonable time line for growth and improvement to occur. The numbers in parentheses correspond with the observations in the commentary that follows the memorandum. A blank professional growth plan with this format is contained in Appendix D.

Professional Growth Plan
School Year 2003-2004

School District ___Surfs Up USD___ Campus ___Fine Elementary___

Teacher ___Susie Doe___ Assignment/Grade ___4th Grade___

1. List area(s) related to the California Standards for the Teaching Profession in which improvement is/are needed. Establish priorities if two or more areas are listed. **(1)**

Standard 1: Engaging and Supporting All Students in Learning

Standard 5: Assessing Student Learning

2. Specify growth activities and dates for completion. **(2)**

a. Attend district cooperative learning workshop on February 1st-2nd. The District will provide a substitute teacher.

b. Observe Mrs. Cathy Coop's class within the next two weeks and schedule an appointment with the supervisor to discuss the observation.

c. Following the workshop and observation in Mrs. Coop's class, develop a lesson plan showing use of cooperative learning strategies.

3. Specify evidence that will be used to determine whether professional growth activities have been completed. **(3)**

a. Provide certificate of completion of district workshop on cooperative learning (due in supervisor's office by February 9th).

b. Schedule a conference with supervisor or consulting teacher to discuss observation in Mrs. Coop's class (no later than February 15th).

c. Submit lesson plan showing cooperative learning strategies (due February 19th) and schedule a time to review its contents with the supervisor and consulting teacher.

4. Specify evidence that will be used to determine whether growth has occurred or is occurring. **(4)**

In future classroom observations, your supervisor and consulting teacher will expect to observe the following:

a. You will solicit student participation and interact with students in such a way that a majority of students are actively and successfully participating in class activities.

b. You will monitor students by moving around the classroom.

c. When students are successful, you will provide positive reinforcement and feedback.

d. When students are not successful or are having difficulty, you will provide prompting and corrective feedback in such a way that students are guided toward successful performances.

_____   _____
Teacher Signature   Date

_____   _____
Consulting Teacher's Signature   Date

_____   _____
Supervisor's Signature   Date

Commentary

(1) This section frames the required improvements within the context of the CSTP.

(2) This section of the PGP directs professional growth *activities*. These directives do not address changes in classroom behavior. They represent the supervisor's and consulting teacher's good faith efforts to assist Ms. Doe in improvement and growth.

(3) This section stipulates the evidence and dates for completion of the growth activities. If the PGP ended here, Ms. Doe could simply attend the workshop, observe in Mrs. Coop's classroom, and submit a written lesson plan. She could successfully complete the growth plan and never address her instructional shortcomings.

(4) This section of the plan establishes the evidence that the supervisor and consulting teacher will use to determine whether Ms. Doe is changing her classroom behavior. If she complies with the directives in the third section but not with those in the fourth, she will not affect student behavior and performance. Finally, notice that directives (a) and (d) in the fourth section follow the format we have recommended: *teacher behavior + linking words —> student behavior.*

WHAT HAPPENS IF THE TEACHER DISAGREES?

The answer to this question will rest, in part, on the provisions of local collective bargaining agreements. Contingent upon bargaining agreement restrictions, the following is a possible scenario that might occur if Ms. Doe from our sample PGP objects to the requirement that she attend a workshop on cooperative learning:

> You explain to Ms. Doe that cooperative learning is a part of the general campus improvement plan, which requires that teachers implement cooperative learning methods and techniques during classroom instruction. Despite your explanation, Ms. Doe remains adamant in her objection to having the training included in the PGP. You then tell her, "I'm sorry that you don't agree. The

emphasis on cooperative learning is an important part of this school's plan for improvement, and I believe that the workshop will help you to learn how to conduct lessons that maximize student involvement in the learning process. Even though you don't agree, I'm still going to include this professional development activity as a requirement in your growth plan."

One might argue the wisdom of requiring Ms. Doe to attend the training against her will, but as a supervisor, your concerns are meeting the requirements of the campus improvement plan and maintaining instructional standards consistent with district policy and the collective bargaining agreement. Therefore, it is appropriate to include the cooperative learning requirement in the PGP. Furthermore, PAR legislation requires school districts to "provide sufficient staff development activities to assist the teacher to improve his or her teaching skills and knowledge" (Educ. Code § 44500 (b)(5)). The directive to attend the cooperative learning workshop complies with this requirement. In addition, the workshop places relatively little burden on Ms. Doe—it occurs during regular school hours, a substitute will be provided, and the cost of the training is paid by the district.

MONITORING GROWTH PLAN ACHIEVEMENT

After the PGP has been developed, the supervisor, and in most cases a peer coach or PAR consulting teacher, will need to monitor the teacher's progress and determine whether the plan's provisions are being met. PAR requirements specify that "assistance and review" of struggling teachers must include "multiple classroom observations . . . during periods of instruction" (Educ. Code § 44500 (b)(3)). These observations should support the teacher's efforts to comply with growth plan directives and measure progress toward its requirements. These classroom visits are best structured as a series of focused classroom observations followed by conferences and focused observation memoranda that provide feedback and support. The following chapters will demonstrate methods that will enable supervisors and consulting teachers to effectively perform these sometimes difficult tasks.

SUMMARY

In writing professional growth plans and directives for improvement, remember the following:

- Give written notice that improvement or change is needed.
- Provide specific written directives for improvement. Make certain that these directives include teacher behavior linked with student behavior.

- Provide assistance and support to demonstrate that you really are trying to help the teacher improve.

- Establish reasonable time lines for growth and improvement to occur. Consider complexity of the changes directed, previous evaluations, years of experience, and type of employment contract in determining a standard for what is reasonable.

- Periodically monitor the teacher's progress toward complying with the terms of the professional growth plan, using the focused observation instruments discussed in Chapter 4 as necessary during classroom observations. Follow-up with written memoranda indicating areas of deficiency. If improvement does not occur, send the teacher a summary memorandum delineating the continuing problems and stating that a recommendation of nonrenewal or termination is likely if improvement is not forthcoming.

- Supervisors should provide written memoranda indicating areas of deficiency and/or improvement after their observation visits.

CHAPTER FIVE: DOCUMENTING ENGAGING AND SUPPORTING ALL STUDENTS IN LEARNING

As noted in the preface, the classroom data-gathering and documentation process described in this and ensuing chapters both complements and is independent of the district's formal teacher appraisal system. It complements local appraisal systems by providing a method to collect data over time. These data can then be factored into an overall teacher evaluation. Evaluators also will want to be certain to adhere to state and district level policies regarding time line requirements and Peer Assistance and Review (PAR) procedures and to sections of the district's collective bargaining agreement that relate to teacher appraisal.

While we approach the classroom documentation process from the point of view of the supervisor in this chapter, the methods we describe should be useful for peer coaches and consulting teachers participating in the PAR intervention process. Peer coaches and consulting teachers should find the focused observation instruments presented in this and subsequent chapters valuable tools when conducting classroom observations. The use of observation instruments linked to the California Standards for the Teaching Profession (CSTP) should better enable consulting teachers to collect objective information about the teaching behaviors of the teachers they support and to relate this information in a manner that reduces the possibility of misunderstanding or conflict. The instruments and the data summary pages that follow them can provide valuable documentation when consulting teachers meet and share information with the teachers they mentor and develop reports for the campus level PAR committee they advise.

While peer coaches and consulting teachers will have frequent and regular opportunities to observe the teachers they mentor, supervisors may have concerns about whether to observe struggling teachers either before or after a professional growth plan (PGP) has been developed. The best approach is to observe the teacher on both occasions. Classroom observation and instructional documentation will assist the supervisor in establishing the need for a PGP as well as the directives it should contain. Once the PGP is in place, it is essential that supervisors document their informal "walk-through" observations in order to assess a teacher's growth with respect to the PGP's directives. If a teacher fails to comply with the plan, a supervisor may later need to develop a summary memorandum indicating his recommendation for contract nonextension (probationary teacher) or termination (permanent teacher). The data collected in pre- and post-PGP observations are an essential component of such a document and will support the supervisor's recommendations should they be challenged.

Similarly, classroom observations should occur both before and after a teacher has been referred for PAR intervention and support. Effective observation and instructional documentation will support the decision to refer a teacher to PAR by identifying deficiencies in classroom performance. Once the teacher has been referred to PAR, it is essential that classroom observations continue. These may be conducted by administrators, consulting teachers, or both. Regardless of who observes the teacher, it is essential that documentation reflects efforts to help the teacher improve and whether the needed improvement takes place.

Our focus in this chapter is the observation, evaluation and documentation of classroom instruction. We emphasize that our primary concern is with the teacher in need of assistance who needs considerable supervisory attention and support. As an evaluator, your task is to transform the information gathered during classroom observations into effective documentation. What follows are guidelines for gathering information from the perspective of a supervisor during a classroom observation, applying Chapter 2's principles of documentation and writing effective memoranda that communicate the content of your observation and your directives for change.

In Chapter 2, Principal Ima Leader documented the out-of-classroom behavior of Bob Instructor, a teacher on her faculty, who disparaged her leadership in a public and unprofessional manner. In addition to publicly criticizing Ima, Bob demonstrated casualness toward his professional responsibilities and often arrived late to school and faculty meetings and failed to attend one meeting. Recall that Ms. Leader wrote a letter of reprimand which carefully omitted reference to Bob's criticism because of the protected nature of his speech, but directly addressed the issue of his tardiness in clear and specific language.

You may recall that Ima Leader also had concerns about Bob's classroom instruction and wondered about the quality of his teaching. It is now the fall of the following school year, and while Bob has improved his attendance habits, his instructional practices still do not meet standards. Early in the year, several students complain that "Mr. Instructor's class is so boring—all we ever do is listen to him and take notes." These complaints motivate Ima's decision to observe Bob in the classroom. This is what she sees:

```
Class:      8th Grade History
Teacher:    Bob Instructor
Date:       9/23/03
Time:       8:30-8:55 a.m. (25 minutes)

Number of students:  24
```

Students are entering room.

Bell rings.

Four students enter after tardy bell. Teacher talks to two students at desk. Teacher does not say anything to four students who enter late.

Teacher: OK, get out your homework papers. We are going to check homework.

Teacher walks around and checks to see if all students have completed homework, making marks in grade book. Two students have nothing on their desks.

Teacher: Put your homework back in your notebooks. We'll go over it later in the period if we have time.

Teacher: OK, take out your handout – last night's reading assignment. Today we're going to be talking about the South after the Civil War, Reconstruction. You were supposed to read this handout as part of last night's assignment. You need to be sure and take notes for the test.

Teacher: Paul, why is this period called Reconstruction?

Paul: No answer

Teacher: OK, Steve, do you know?

Steve: Because the North rebuilt the Southern cities it has destroyed?

Teacher: No, not exactly. Mariana, do you know?

Mariana: I'm not sure, but I think it was because the Radical Republicans believed that the Southern leadership had violated the Constitution and needed to be reeducated and required some kind of pledge of loyalty to the United States. Also because they were rebuilding, you know, the farms and factories.

Teacher: That's a good answer. Did everybody get that?

Teacher is standing behind the lectern. Teacher begins to talk about Reconstruction. Tells students who leaders were, what the dates were, and writes three significant things the Radical Republicans did on the board. (He writes: 1.disenfranchized southern leaders, 2. established the freedman's bureu, 3. imposed heavy taxes on Southern landowners).

Teacher: Now, Audrey, why did they disenfranchise the Southerners?

Audrey: I don't know.

Teacher: Why not? Didn't you read the assignment?

Teacher: Aaron?

Aaron: What's disenfranchise? *(student mispronounces word)*

Teacher: Look it up.

Teacher: Mariana, can you bail him out?

Mariana: They disenfranchised them so that the Northerners could control who got elected to public office.

Teacher: Right again, Mariana.

Nari: *(Reading from the handout)* What's a permutation?

Teacher: *(Ignoring the question)* You guys better be paying attention and taking notes because this stuff is going to be on the test Friday.

Teacher: All right, Aaron, I'm going to give you another chance. What was the difference between Federal fiscal policy in different Southern states?

Aaron:	Well, they were less physical in some states than they were in others. I mean, they didn't push the people in Virginia around like they did the ones in Mississippi and Georgia.
Teacher:	Not hardly. Does anybody know? *(Aaron puts the handout in his folder and puts down his pen)*
	Pause. No hands are raised. Teacher still standing at lectern.
Teacher:	Didn't anybody read the assignment?
	Mariana raises her hand.
Mariana:	The tax burden in Virginia was much lower than it was in other Southern States and because of that, fewer people lost their land and fewer carpetbaggers moved in to buy it at tax sales.
Teacher:	I'm glad at least one person read the assignment.
	Teacher begins to discuss military policy during Recon-struction.
	Six students are taking notes — all others are not taking notes.
	Teacher continues to stand at lectern.
	Three students in the back (Aaron, Paul, Gadhi) are whispering.
	Teacher still at lectern talking about military policy.
Teacher:	And why were the former Southern troops assigned the job of fighting Indians on the frontier? Matt?
Matt:	I'm sorry, what?
Teacher:	You sure are. Paul?
Paul:	Why were Southerners what?
Teacher:	Assigned to fight Indians on the frontier.
Paul:	Because they were suspicious of the Southerners' loyalty and didn't trust them to serve in other places, like outside the South.
Teacher:	Right, Paul. See what happens when you pay attention.

Observation ends at 8:55. Teacher is still at lectern and discussing Reconstruction. Jesse is helping Nari sort papers. Kevin and Jasmine are talking. Two students are watching me. Mariana and Paul appear to be listening and taking notes.

While Ima was able to observe all that is included in our script of Bob's lesson, it is unlikely that she could have fully recorded it all. She might have jotted notes on a paper or used a form, checking boxes or circling numbers in order to rate Bob's performance, but to Ima neither of these methods is very effective because they omit so much of what she observes.

TYPES OF CLASSROOM OBSERVATIONS

Most of the data collection related to documenting instruction will come from classroom observations. The most common classroom observation is the so-called "bell-to-bell observation" in which an evaluator observes a full class period from the beginning of a lesson to the end. This kind of observation is usually required for formal teacher evaluation procedures. Generally speaking, a full class period observation may be needed:

- to fulfill the requirements of formal district teacher appraisal systems;

- for a Peer Assistance and Review (PAR) consulting teacher to gain more complete information about a referred teacher;

- when the evaluator needs to consider a wide range of teacher and student behaviors; and

- to assess the requirements of an extensive professional growth plan.

While the full class period observations permit evaluators to gather a significant amount of information, they require a considerable commitment in time. Clearly there are practical limitations to how many full class observations a busy administrator or consulting teacher will be able to complete for any one teacher. Recall that state law requires a formal assessment be conducted at least once each year for probationary teachers and at least every other year for permanent status teachers.

It is good professional practice to hold a formal post-observation conference with the teacher following a full class period observation. State law favors this kind of communication with teachers. In the context of the overall evaluation, it requires that a conference must be held between the teacher being evaluated and the evaluator before the last school day of the year (Educ. Code § 44663).

A second kind of classroom observation is commonly referred to as a "walk-through." Some walk-throughs may be 3-5 minutes in length while others may be 15-30 minutes long. These shorter observations enable a supervisor or consulting teacher to observe more frequently in an individual classroom and/or in more total classrooms. The 3-5 minute walk-through is useful when a supervisor or consulting teacher wants to:

- get general sense of the teacher's classroom;

- initially investigate a complaint from a student, teacher, or parent;

- get a sense of a single instructional issue such as inappropriate student behavior or the level of student participation;

- monitor district requirements such as the use of manipulatives in teaching mathematics or reducing the amount of time students are assigned low-level, paper/pencil tasks.

A 3-5 minute walk-through can only provide a superficial sense of instructional issues or problems. Supervisors and consulting teachers must spend more time in the classroom in order to gain a more complete understanding of teacher effectiveness and student learning.

The 15-30 minute walk-through is a useful compromise between the full class observation and the 3-5 minute walk-through. The 15-30 minute walk-through observation is useful when a supervisor, peer coach, or consulting teacher wants to:

- focus data collection on a single standard of the district's teacher evaluation system or the California Standards for the Teaching Profession (CSTP);

- monitor the requirements of a professional growth plan or the directives incorporated in a written memorandum;

- efficiently gather data over an extended period of time to show a pattern of behavior; or

- gather additional information as a follow-up to a full classroom observation.

Practically speaking, over the course of a school year most evaluators will encounter circumstances that require each type of observation. Regardless of the length of observation, it is imperative that evaluators collect accurate information about the classroom's they observe.

METHODS OF GATHERING DATA IN CLASSROOM OBSERVATION

Effective classroom observations are a prerequisite for effective documentation of instruction, so it is important that principals such as Ima and other administrators charged with evaluation duties are able to effectively collect information in the classroom. In addition, classroom observation is an integral component of the PAR process, so it is also important for consulting teachers to understand methods of gathering data during their frequent classroom visits.

There are four primary methods of gathering and recording information during an observation: scripting, writing an anecdotal record, electronic recording, and using focused observation instruments. Let's briefly consider each of these methods.

Scripting

A script is a word-for-word transcript of what the teacher and students say. If Ima chose to employ the scripting technique when observing Bob, her notes might read:

Mr. I.:   OK, take out your handout – last night's reading assignment. Today we're going to be talking about the South after the Civil War, Reconstruction. You were supposed to read this handout as part of last night's assignment. You need to be sure and take notes for the test. Paul, why is this period called "Reconstruction"?

Paul: I don't know.

Mr. I.:   OK. Steve, do you know?

Steve: Because the North rebuilt the Southern cities it had destroyed.

Mr. I.:   No, not exactly. Mariana, do you know?

Scripting is useful when you are conducting a lengthy classroom observation which will result in decisions about varied aspects of the teaching and learning process. For example, Ima might be considering many aspects of Mr. Instructor's instruction—whether his students actively participate, are successful and engaged in the lesson; or whether Bob incorporates classroom management strategies, aligns instruction with district/state curriculum standards, has created an effective environment for learning, and so on. Scripting is a good option when you need an encompassing and detailed record of everything that was said and done during the lesson.

One advantage of scripting's detailed word-for-word account of the lesson is that it may clearly highlight the reasons the lesson was or was not successful. The disadvantages of scripting are obvious. You may be so busy writing (with your head down, most likely) that you may miss important non-verbal student and teacher behavior. You also might find that completeness and accuracy are very difficult to attain.

Anecdotal Record

Writing an anecdotal record differs from scripting in that the evaluator takes descriptive notes about what is observed rather than trying to record each word. The exchange in the example above would appear this way if written as an anecdotal record:

```
Mr. Instructor told students to take out handout and to take notes.
Called on Paul and Steve.  Neither knew the answer.  No corrective
feedback.
```

Like scripting, the anecdotal record is useful when you are conducting a lengthy classroom observation which will be the basis for many decisions and for which you will need information about many aspects of the lesson. It is appropriate to use anecdotal records rather than scripting when you do not need a verbatim record of the teacher monologue and student/teacher interaction.

Taking notes for the anecdotal record is faster and easier than scripting, allows the observer to note non-verbal teacher and student behaviors, and provides a great deal of information about many different aspects of the teaching/learning process. On the other hand, it does not provide an exact record of what teachers and students say.

Electronic Recording

Electronic recording can occur in a teacher's classroom only with the permission of the teacher and principal (Educ. Code § 51512). State law also permits a teacher to record himself/herself without approval for the purposes of improving instruction (Educ. Code § 44034). Always check with the district's human relations department to determine whether or not electronic recording is permitted (even with the teacher's permission) by district policy or by the collective bargaining contract.

Depending on the legality of electronic recording in your district, you may choose to record a lesson with audio or video equipment when the observation will be lengthy, when it will form the basis for many decisions, and when you need incontrovertible evidence of what was said or done during the lesson. You may also choose to record electronically when you decide that your skills at scripting or note-taking are not good enough to give you the information you need.

An advantage of electronic recording is that it provides a word-for-word record of the lesson with detailed verbal (and with video, nonverbal) information for use in analyzing the lesson and its effectiveness. You also have incontrovertible proof of what occurred in the classroom.

There are several disadvantages of electronic recording. To begin with, the video or audio recording equipment available in schools is often of poor quality. Audio recording omits critical non-verbal behaviors while video recording sees only what the camera beholds (and the camera is often pointed at the wrong place). Another very important drawback to electronic recording is that the disruption created by the equipment in the classroom is greater than that created by the observer alone. Moreover, the presence of the equipment may aggravate the teacher's anxiety and resistance.

Focused Observation Instruments

Suppose Ima wants to visit Mr. Instructor's class specifically to observe how his students participate. She has concerns that Bob is not meeting the first standard of the CSTP, which deals with student participation. Because Ima is not concerned with a full range of instructional issues, she chooses to use a focused observation instrument.

What is a focused observation instrument? It is a data gathering form that targets a particular area of teaching weakness, does not require a great deal of writing, and is easy to complete. Because focused observation instruments target a limited range of classroom behaviors, they generally enable evaluators to collect more detailed information. Many California school districts include focused observation instruments as part of their teacher evaluation process. We reviewed many such instruments in preparing this handbook. While some district instruments facilitated effective classroom observation, many that we reviewed were simple checklists that omitted a great deal of relevant information about teacher and student behaviors.

The focused observation instruments we present in this handbook are tailored to the California Standards for the Teaching Profession and are rooted in the current and best research on effective teaching behaviors. They are structured to simplify effective observation while enabling the observer to collect a wealth of information about the teaching behaviors he observes. In addition, they are designed to smooth the transition from classroom observation to the documentation of instruction. Readers will find blank versions of the instruments in Appendix A. We have modified the copyright for this handbook so that readers may copy the instruments for their own use.

Ima's instrument (she uses the instrument on page 5-12) enables her to collect a significant amount of data about how students participate in Bob's classroom. Because she is not busy recording other deficiencies, Ima is able to note which students participate, the nature of their participation, and whether they are successful or not. In so doing, she is able to record Bob's teaching behaviors and how they affect his students' engagement in the lesson. Because of the narrow range of behaviors the instrument considers, Ima recognizes that the instrument is not appropriate for her formal evaluation of Mr. Instructor. But on less formal classroom visits such as this one, the instrument enables her to identify specific areas of weakness and helps her to make decisions about how best to direct Bob to improve his teaching practices.

GATHERING DATA IN THE CLASSROOM OF THE TEACHER NEEDING ASSISTANCE

In Chapter 3 we described the teacher in need of assistance and made a series of recommendations for appropriate supervision practices. Recall that the teacher in need of assistance has some competence but also has some deficiencies in instructional practice. These deficiencies impede his effectiveness and may have negative effects on student behavior and achievement.

In the California framework for teacher evaluation and assistance, a teacher in need of assistance such as Bob is generally referred for PAR support after an unsatisfactory final evaluation. The legislation that implemented PAR in 1999, Assembly Bill 1X, requires that veteran teachers receiving unsatisfactory evaluations participate in the PAR process. The PAR legislation grants districts considerable discretion about many of the details of PAR implementation, but it clearly requires that multiple classroom observations form the core of the Peer Assistance and Review process (Educ. Code § 44500 (b)(3)).

Ima is well aware of PAR's requirements and plans to refer Bob for PAR assistance. With this in mind, she plans to conduct several informal observations in his classroom to give her a clearer picture of his deficiencies. Ima's informal visits consist of a series of fifteen-to-twenty minute observations in which she focuses her data collection efforts on the areas in which he exhibits weakness. She structures her data gathering according to the CSTP, which provide a useful framework for categorizing teaching behaviors. Because of the short and informal nature of these observations, Ima chooses to use one of the focused observation instruments presented in this handbook on each visit.

Each instrument addresses one of the first five standards of the CSTP. These standards include:

1. Engaging and Supporting All Students in Learning
2. Creating and Maintaining Effective Environments for Student Learning
3. Understanding and Organizing Subject Matter for Student Learning
4. Planning Instruction and Designing Learning Experiences for All Students
5. Assessing Student Learning

The sixth standard, Developing as a Professional Educator, is not specifically related to classroom behaviors and is beyond the scope of this handbook.

In this and the remaining chapters, we present the six focused observation instruments. Each instrument is tailored to one of the five "Standards" listed above. We demonstrate the use of five of the instruments using a brief observation of Bob Instructor's lesson on Civil War Reconstruction.

The California standards and our focused observation instruments are rooted in some of the best research on effective teaching behaviors. We include a bibliography of this research in Appendix E. Our focus in this chapter is the first CSTP standard: Engaging and Supporting All Students in Learning. The table (Figure 5-1 on the opposite page) explicates the research related to each component of the first standard with respect to observable teacher and student behaviors.

ENGAGING AND SUPPORTING ALL STUDENTS IN LEARNING

As we noted earlier, the documentation of instruction can be simplified by using a focused observation instrument that focuses on a narrow range of instructional behaviors.

Before entering Mr. Instructor's classroom, Ima decides which of the five standards she wants to document and selects the appropriate instrument. In this way, she avoids the difficulties of scripting and other means of recording, and her documentation will be specific and relevant to the issue she wants to address. Ima knows that when a teacher such as Bob has many instructional problems, it is best to focus first on the area in which he has the most potential for positive change. In so doing, she provides him with the greatest opportunity for improvement and reduces the likelihood that he will become frustrated and demoralized.

Using a Focused Observation Instrument to Gather and Record Data

Ima decides that the best place to begin with Bob is Standard 1: Engaging and Supporting All Students in Learning, and she uses the focused observation instrument tailored to this standard from this handbook. What follows is Ima's completed instrument from Mr. Instructor's class on Reconstruction (as previously noted, a blank copy of each instrument is contained in Appendix A). Notice that there are numbers in parentheses on each of the forms. These numbers correspond with comments pertaining to each part of the instrument that follow in the commentary section.

Figure 5-1

Standard One
ENGAGING AND SUPPORTING ALL STUDENTS IN LEARNING

1-1 CONNECTING STUDENTS' PRIOR KNOWLEDGE, LIFE EXPERIENCE, AND INTERESTS WITH LEARNING GOALS

The teacher:
- reviews the content of previous lessons in establishing the context for current instruction.
- organizes instruction, examples and materials to relate to student interests and needs.
- uses positive motivational statements to challenge and encourage students.
- builds on students' questions to extend their knowledge and understanding.

Students:
- are able to connect new material to prior knowledge.
- are attentive, interested and engaged in on-task behaviors.
- connect learning to their lives and experiences.
- provide feedback and ask questions.

1-2 USING A VARIETY OF INSTRUCTIONAL STRATEGIES AND RESOURCES TO RESPOND TO STUDENTS' DIVERSE NEEDS

The teacher:
- engages students in a variety of activities that accommodate different learning styles.
- structures questions to maximize student success.
- varies the cognitive level of questions according to student ability level.
- organizes lessons to include varied activities and materials.

Students:
- actively participate.
- are engaged in class discussion and complete activities.

1-3 FACILITATING LEARNING EXPERIENCES THAT PROMOTE AUTONOMY, INTERACTION AND CHOICE

The teacher:
- provides students with opportunities for independent and collaborative learning.
- assists students in managing time and making decisions.
- conveys an expectation of student attention and cooperation.
- monitors and supports student learning.

Students:
- provide feedback and volunteer responses.
- are on-task during activities.
- are responsible and use time productively.
- work collaboratively and make independent decisions.

1-4 ENGAGING STUDENTS IN PROBLEM SOLVING, CRITICAL THINKING, AND OTHER ACTIVITIES THAT MAKE SUBJECT MATTER MEANINGFUL

The teacher:
- incorporates meaningful problem solving, application, analysis, and evaluation activities into the lesson.
- engages students in discussion and application activities.
- provides opportunities for all students to practice skills and concepts.
- monitors and supports students in problem solving, analysis and evaluation activities.
- encourages the development of multiple perspectives and alternative solutions.

Students:
- are engaged in critical thinking and problem solving activities.
- solve problems in different ways and present multiple points of view.
- ask questions and consider different perspectives.

1-5 PROMOTING SELF-DIRECTED, REFLECTIVE LEARNING FOR ALL STUDENTS

The teacher:
- encourages students to initiate their own learning.
- provides opportunities for students to work collaboratively and to learn from their peers.
- emphasizes student responsibility for work.
- helps students to develop strategies for learning.

Students:
- initiate learning.
- have opportunities to monitor themselves during instruction.
- volunteer, provide feedback and make choices.
- are on-task during autonomous activities.
- are responsible and use time productively.

FOCUSED OBSERVATION INSTRUMENT #1

Engaging and Supporting All Students In Learning

Name of Teacher: __Bob Instructor__   Date of Observation: __9/23/03__

Subject/Grade Level: __8th/History__   Time of Observation: Begin: __8:30__

Specific Content/Activity: End: __8:55__   **(1)**

__Civil War/Reconstruction__   Number of Students in Class: __24__

Learning Objective: "Today, we're going to be talking about the South after the Civil War, Reconstruction."

Record the names (descriptions, seat assignment) of students who were assessed. Circle the + beside the name(s) of students whose participation was succussful. Circle the – beside the name(s) of students whose participation was not successful. Record the teacher's response to the student's response/performance/demonstration.

STUDENT	QUESTION	SUCCESSFUL/ UNSUCCESSFUL	TEACHER RESPONSE TO STUDENT
1. Paul	"Why is this period called Reconstruction?"	+ ⊝ ?	"OK. Steve, do you know?" **(2)**
2. Steve	"OK. Steve, do you know?"	+ ⊝ ?	"No, not exactly. Mariana, do you know?"
3. Mariana	"Mariana, do you know?"	⊕ – ?	"That's a good answer. Did everybody get that?"
4. Audrey	"Why did they disenfranchise the Southerners?"	+ ⊝ ?	"Didn't you read the assignment?" (calls on Aaron)
5. Aaron	(same question to Aaron)	+ ⊝ ?	(student asks for definition of disenfranchisement) "Look it up." (calls on Mariana)
6. Mariana	(same question to Mariana)	⊕ – ?	"Right again, Mariana. You guys better be paying attention because this stuff is going to be on the test." (calls on Aaron: "I'm going to give you another chance.")
7. Aaron	"What was the difference between Federal fiscal policy and fiscal policy in other Southern states?"	+ ⊝ ?	"Not hardly, Aaron. Does anybody know?" (Aaron puts handout in folder and puts down pen. Mr. I. calls on Mariana)
8. Mariana	(same question to Mariana)	⊕ – ?	"I'm glad one person read the assignment, Mariana." (Mr. I. continues to lecture)
9. Matt	"Why were former Southern troops assigned the job of fighting Indians on the frontier?"	+ ⊝ ?	(following Mr. I.'s question, Matt asks, "I'm sorry, what?") "You sure are." Mr. I. then calls on Paul)
10. Paul	(same question to Paul)	⊕ – ?	"Right, Paul. See what happens when you pay attention?"

Note: Teacher stood behind lectern for entire period.

Instructional Strategies Used to Promote and Support Student Engagement

Check any techniques that the teacher uses to promote active, successful student engagement in learning. Checking the technique does not necessarily mean that the technique was used effectively—it simply means that the technique was used. Write notes or comments that will help you to remember what the teacher did/failed to do.

(3)

_____ The teacher facilitates connections between new knowledge and prior knowledge, other subject areas and/or students' own experiences.

_____ The teacher reviews the content of previous lessons in establishing the context for current instruction.

_____ The teacher provides opportunities for students to volunteer, offer feedback and make independent choices.

X The teacher provides frequent opportunities for students to actively participate in the lesson. _Called on 6 students_

_____ The teacher structures questions to maximize student success.

_____ The teacher varies the cognitive level of questions to accommodate students of different ability levels.

X The teacher positively reinforces student participation and success. _Reinforced Mariana's responses_

_____ The teacher encourages slow/reluctant learners.

_____ Instructional activities and materials are varied.

_____ Instructional activities and materials relate to students' interests and needs.

_____ Instructional activities allow/encourage students to interact with each other.

_____ Instructional activities include opportunities for independent student practice.

_____ Instructional activities emphasize problem solving, critical thinking, analysis, and/or other higher order thinking skills.

_____ Other technique(s)

Summary of Data and Evaluation of Student Engagement and Learning

In the space below, summarize the data from the previous two pages and evaluate the level of instructional support for student engagement and learning.

(4)

Active Student Participation and Success

1. How many students participated? _6_ of _24_ participated.

2. How many students were successful? _2_ of _6_ who participated.

3. How many students were unsuccessful? _4_ of _6_ who participated.

What was the learning objective?

"Today, we're going to be talking about the South after the Civil War, Reconstruction."

What instructional activities, strategies, and resources were implemented in teaching the lesson?

Lecturing and random questioning.

Based on the data, which statements best describe what you observed?

The number(s) in parentheses indicate the component of the first standard that is or is not being met.

Meets Standards	Does Not Meet Standards
____ All/almost all students were engaged and successful (all components).	_X_ Few/no students were engaged and successful (all components).
____ All/almost all students successfully made connections to prior knowledge, to other subject areas and to interests and experiences outside the classroom (1-1).	_X_ Few/no students successfully made connections to prior knowledge, to other subject areas and to interests and experiences outside the classroom (1-1).
____ All/almost all students successfully participated in problem solving, critical thinking and application activities (1-4).	_X_ Few/no students successfully participated in problem solving, critical thinking and application activities (1-4).
____ All/almost all students engaged in self-directed/self-motivated learning (1-5).	_X_ Few/no students engaged in self-directed/self-motivated learning (1-5).
____ All/almost all students experienced opportunities for autonomous interaction and choice (1-3).	_X_ Few/no students experienced opportunities for autonomous interaction and choice (1-3).
____ Instruction incorporated a variety of strategies, activities and materials related to students' interests and needs (1-2).	_X_ Instruction did not incorporate a variety of strategies, activities and materials related to students' interests and needs (1-2).
____ Instructional activities accommodated students of varying cognitive abilities (1-2).	_X_ Instructional activities did not accommodate students of varying cognitive abilities (1-2).

Commentary

(1) The first section of the instrument provides essential information that Ima will need when she is ready to write her memorandum to Mr. Instructor, (e.g., date and time of the observation, length of the observations, etc.).

(2) In this section, she records each teacher/student interaction as it occurs. Paul's response was incorrect and Mr. Instructor called on Steve. When Steve answered incorrectly, Mr. Instructor called on Mariana. Mariana's response was correct and Mr. Instructor told her that she had a "good answer." When Audrey did not know an answer, Mr. Instructor asked, "Why not? Didn't you read the assignment?"

Note: All information is presented in objective, non-judgmental terms. Avoid writing judgmental or editorial comments. When Mr. Instructor responds to Audrey, "Why not? Didn't you read the assignment?" write down his exact words rather than the inappropriate judgment "put-down comment by teacher." In recording observation data and writing documentation, stick to the facts.

(3) This section of the instrument is completed in the classroom during "down time," that is, when there are few teacher/student interactions and when Ima has time to consider other things happening in the classroom.

The form indicates by check mark notations that the teacher used random calling and called on six students. Use of positive reinforcement also is checked, with the added note that Mariana's responses were reinforced. You may *later* make the judgment whether or not these techniques were effective. During the observation, however, she only records that these techniques were used, regardless of whether or not they were used appropriately or effectively.

(4) The final part of the focused observation instrument should be completed outside of the classroom. It consists of a summary of the data and judgments from the previous two sections of the instrument. Remember that the preceding data were factual and objective — no judgments were made about the quality or effectiveness of the teaching behaviors. In completing this section, Ima may both *summarize* the data and *make judgments* about the teacher's performance. In the case of Mr. Instructor, the summary reveals the following:

- Six of the twenty-four students participated.
- Two of the six who participated were successful. Three of the four correct responses came from Mariana. The observer is concerned with how many *students* gave correct responses, not with how many responses were correct.
- Most questions were at the application level or above on Bloom's Cognitive Taxonomy; however, only two of twenty-four students (Mariana and Paul) were successful.
- None of the questions connected the new learning to other disciplines or to issues beyond the classroom.

The sections labeled "Meets Standard" and "Does Not Meet Standard" provide a contrast of judgments based on the data from the observation.

Writing a Focused Observation Memorandum

Ima is now ready to write a memorandum to communicate what she observed and her recommendations to Mr. Instructor. This memorandum will serve as a record of the information if it is needed to develop a professional growth plan or to demonstrate non-compliance with a previously developed plan. In the case of Mr. Instructor, a growth plan has not been developed yet; therefore, Ima sends him a focused observation memorandum, incorporating the information she gathered during her classroom visit.

Directives for professional development activities and changes in behavior are essential in a professional growth plan but are not required in a focused observation memorandum. Ima may choose to include them in her focused observation memorandum if she believes that Bob's deficiencies can be remedied without a formal growth plan. Ima chooses to include directives in her memorandum to Bob. You can see this in her sample memorandum on the following pages.

The following is a checklist for the components of a focused observation memorandum related to instruction.

Checklist for Instructional Documentation

___ Use district or campus letterhead paper.

___ Include date memorandum was written.

___ Include date and time of the classroom observation (important in demonstrating that you have not singled out one time of the day or one group of students).

___ Include number of students in the class (especially important when dealing with issues such as active participation and student success).

___ Set forth your findings of fact resulting from the data gathered during the classroom observation. These should be written in objective, factual language and without judgment.

___ State your conclusions or judgments regarding what happened. Anchor them, whenever possible, in the district or campus criteria for effective instruction. For example, "These data indicate that your teaching did not meet district expectations for evaluating and providing feedback on student progress during instruction."

___ If you choose, include any directives regarding expected future conduct and remedial activities that the employee is required to undertake. (See guidelines for writing instructional directives in Chapter 4.)

___ Give the employee an opportunity to respond.

___ Require the dated signature of the employee or a third party witness.

Using the data from the stuctured observation instrument, Ima's focused observation memorandum might look like this:

Surfs Up Unified School District
1234 Sunny Lane
Surfs Up, CA 90000

TO: Mr. Bob Instructor
FROM: Dr. Ima Leader
DATE: September 29, 2003
SUBJECT: Report of Classroom Observation

This memorandum will formally communicate information gathered during my observation of September 23, 2003. I observed from 8:30 to 8:55 while you were conducting a lesson on Civil War Reconstruction with a group of 24 eighth graders.

The observation revealed the following information.

1. The learning objective was stated as, "Today we're going to be talking about the South after the Civil War, Reconstruction."

2. Six of 24 students participated (Paul, Steve, Mariana, Audrey, Aaron, and Matt).

3. Two of the six who participated were successful (Paul and Mariana).

4. The lesson was in a lecture/discussion format in which you presented information and asked questions to six of the 24 students.

5. While most questions were at the application level or higher on Bloom's taxonomy ("Why. . . ?" and "What is the difference. . . ?"), most students were not successful in responding to the questions.

6. Instructional strategies did not include students successfully connecting the learning about Reconstruction with other disciplines or with issues beyond the classroom.

The first standard of the California Standards for the Teaching Profession and the Surfs Up U.S.D. appraisal system has an expectation for active, successful student participation in the learning process. Within that standard there is an expectation that most students are actively engaged in problem solving, critical thinking and other activities that make the subject matter meaningful. In addition there is an expectation that students are able to connect new learning within the discipline, with other disciplines, and/or with issues beyond the classroom.

Based on the data collected during my observation, these expectations are not being met. These observations have prompted me to refer you for PAR intervention and support. Surfs Up U.S.D. values you as a professional, and it my goal as an instructional leader to provide you with the best resources in the interest of improving instruction for all students. It is my hope that you will begin your participation in the PAR process with this goal in mind.

I will be back some time during the first week in December to observe your instruction. During that observation and all future observations in your classroom, I will expect to observe:

1. Most students actively and successfully participating in the learning process;

2. Most students successfully participating in problem solving, critical thinking and/or other application activities;

3. Students making connections of new learning with prior/future learning in history, with other disciplines, and/or with issues beyond the classroom.

Copy: PAR Council

My signature verifies that I have received a copy of this memorandum. It does not necessarily mean that I agree with the content. I understand that I have the right to present a written response within ten working days.

_____   _____
/s/ Bob Instructor   Date

NOTE: This memorandum contains comprehensive directives for changes in behavior and professional growth activities. The directives are written in the form described in Chapter 4. While such comprehensive directives are not essential in a focused observation memorandum, you may choose to include them for the reasons previously expressed.

LEARNER-CENTERED INSTRUCTION

The increased emphasis placed on learner-centered instruction has reshaped the way in which many teachers structure their lessons and organize student activities. During learner-centered instruction, students direct their own learning and support the learning of their classmates by working in groups or pairs. Because the teacher is not the focus during these activities, evaluators may find the instrument presented on the next page to be a useful tool in assessing student progress during learner centered-instruction.

The instrument resembles a seating chart. Evaluators should enter a student name at the top of each square and block the squares to reflect student groupings. In each box the evaluator will record the student-student exchanges as well as student interactions with the teacher. Evaluators may wish to incorporate a notation system that enables them to recognize when students are successful and when they aren't. A frequently used system employs the notations of (✓+) for successful participation and (✓-) for students who are unsuccessful. In addition, evaluators are advised to make notes about whether students are engaged in on-task behavior and the content of their discussions as well as the teacher's response to students' questions, performances, and behavior.

These observations can then be summarized on the form entitled "Summary of Data and Evaluation of Student Engagement and Learning" included as the fourth section of the previous instrument.

Learner Centered Instruction

Name of Teacher: _____

Subject/Grade Level: _____

Specific Content/Activity:

Date of Observation: _____

Time of Observation: Begin: _____

End: _____

Number of Students in Class: _____

Learning Objective:

Document the active participation of students. Enter ✓+ if the student was successful and ✓- if the student was unsuccessful. Use arrows to record student-student exchanges as well as teacher-student dialogue. Make notes to jog your memory about the content of discussion and teacher responses to students' questions, performances, and behavior.

SUMMARY

In this chapter we have presented an overview of classroom data collection methods, introduced the use of focused observation instruments, and demonstrated how to document instruction through the use of a focused observation instrument. While our discussion has been largely from the supervisory point of view, focused observation instruments are also useful tools for peer coaches and consulting teachers. In the following chapters, we will expand our discussion of the focused observation instruments to include their use in mentoring relationships, and we will present instruments tailored to the remaining standards of the CSTP.

CHAPTER SIX: DOCUMENTING CLASSROOM MANAGEMENT AND THE LEARNING ENVIRONMENT

In this chapter we will address gathering classroom observation data and documenting instruction with respect to the second standard of the California Standards for the Teaching Profession (CSTP): Creating and Maintaining Effective Environments for Student Learning. This standard encompasses issues related to management of student behavior, effective use of instructional time, and the affective environment of the classroom.

As we previously have noted, the CSTP and our focused observation instruments are based on the current and best research on effective teaching. A bibliography of the research behind the focused observation instruments presented in this handbook can be found in Appendix E. The table (Figure 6-1 on the next page) presents the research related to each component of the second standard in terms of teacher and student behaviors.

CREATING AND MAINTAINING EFFECTIVE ENVIRONMENTS FOR STUDENT LEARNING

Using a Focused Observation Instrument to Gather and Record Data

Effective classroom management is a prerequisite for good teaching and student learning. Disorderly classrooms, disruptive students and disorganized teachers handicap the learning process and impede student achievement.

You will recall that in Chapter 5 Principal Ima Leader observed Bob Instructor's classroom and documented her evaluation of his instructional practices for the first CSTP standard, Engaging Students in Learning. Now suppose that Ima has concerns that Bob's classroom management skills are lacking and that the learning environment in his classroom has declined substantially. She has noticed that Bob manages class time poorly, is not attentive to students' off-task and inappropriate behavior, and does not enforce either campus or classroom rules.

In addition to poor classroom management practices, Ima is concerned about how Bob interacts with students, particularly those students who are not quickly successful or who have difficulty with learning. She plans a classroom observation in which she will focus her data collection on these issues. To help her in this task, she chooses the focused observation instrument tailored to the second standard of the CSTP. The instrument presents statements that reflect learning environments that do and do not meet each component of the second standard. Ima checks the boxes that reflect what she observes.

Unlike the other focused observation instruments we present, this instrument calls for some judgments to be made during the observation. The nature of the "learning environment" is more subjective than many other areas of classroom instruction. It is, therefore, important that Ima records notes that support the statements she has checked. She may choose to include direct quotations from the teacher and students as well as anecdotal information about teacher and student behavior in the "Notes" column.

What follows is Ima's completed focused observation instrument from Mr. Instructor's class on Reconstruction (see Chapter 5's script of the lesson). (A blank copy of this instrument is included in Appendix A.) Notice that there are numbers in parentheses in each section of the form. These numbers correspond with the comments in the commentary that follows.

Figure 6-1

Standard Two

CREATING AND MAINTAINING EFFECTIVE ENVIRONMENTS FOR STUDENT LEARNING

2-1 CREATING A PHYSICAL ENVIRONMENT THAT ENGAGES ALL STUDENTS

The teacher:
- arranges and changes the classroom as necessary in order to facilitate instruction.
- plans student seating in order to maximize the level of participation.
- does not permit disruptive talking, noise or interruptions during teacher-directed instruction.
- anticipates critical problems and organizes the classroom and instruction to eliminate the conditions conducive to their occurrence.

Students:
- are able to move through the classroom with a minimum of disruption.
- are able to access materials and resources.
- are able to view instructional areas clearly.
- are not disruptive.

2-2 ESTABLISHING A CLIMATE THAT PROMOTES FAIRNESS AND RESPECT

The teacher:
- encourages student participation and respects student's contributions to the class.
- has frequent positive interactions with students and responds in a supportive manner.
- actively elicits the participation of low-achieving students.
- responds to inappropriate behavior.

Students:
- demonstrate respectful attitudes toward the teacher and other students.

2-3 PROMOTING SOCIAL DEVELOPMENT AND GROUP RESPONSIBILITY

The teacher:
- emphasizes student responsibility for productive use of time and completion of work.
- develops and implements procedures to keep students accountable for their work.
- maintains an expectation of student attention, cooperation and responsibility in working toward the completion of assignments.

Students:
- have opportunities to work with one another.
- demonstrate respect for the opinions and perspectives of students who are different from themselves.
- are responsible for their work.

2-4 ESTABLISHING AND MAINTAINING STANDARDS FOR STUDENT BEHAVIOR

The teacher:
- enforces rules and procedures consistently.
- clarifies the standards for student behavior, provides a rationale for these standards, and explains the consequences of inappropriate behavior.
- monitors student behavior and intervenes when inappropriate or disruptive behavior occurs.
- provides specific feedback regarding the appropriateness of student behavior.
- helps students to resolve their own problems and conflicts.
- uses student misbehavior as an opportunity to teach appropriate behavior.
- provides praise for correct behavior.
- uses a variety of verbal and nonverbal signals to stop inappropriate behavior.

Students:
- are aware of and adhere to classroom rules and procedures.
- remain on task.
- are able to solve problems and resolve conflicts.

2-5 PLANNING AND IMPLEMENTING CLASSROOM PROCEDURES AND ROUTINES THAT SUPPORT STUDENT LEARNING

The teacher:
- establishes, posts, teaches (and reteaches as needed) classroom routines and procedures.
- structures activities and uses cues in order to maintain appropriate pacing and student engagement.
- provides clear directions during transitions between activities.
- maintains and reinforces student engagement and identifies and helps those students who do not understand the instructions.
- actively involves students in the lesson and is quick to respond to off-task behaviors.

Students:
- follow classroom procedures and are aware of established routines.
- remain seated during instruction and engage in appropriate behavior.
- remain on task.

2-6 USING INSTRUCTIONAL TIME EFFECTIVELY

The teacher:
- begins promptly and provides rapid and smooth transitions between activities.
- makes full use of instructional time and minimizes interruptions and transition time.

Students:
- are engaged in learning activities during instructional time.
- have adequate time to complete activities.
- remain engaged in instructional activities.

FOCUSED OBSERVATION INSTRUMENT #2

Creating and Maintaining Effective Environments for Student Learning

Name of Teacher: Bob Instructor

Subject/Grade Level: 8th/History

Specific Content/Activity: Handout

Date of Observation: 9/23/03

Time of Observation: Begin: 8:30

End: 8:55

Number of Students in Class: 24

(1)

The statements on the left reflect effective learning environments that meet standards, and those on the right reflect learning environments that do not meet standards. Check the statements that best describe your observations. Include notes that detail and/or support your observations.

Creating a Physical Environment that Engages All Students

(2)

Meets Standards	Does Not Meet Standards	Notes
X The classroom environment is orderly and safe.	____ The classroom environment is disorderly and/or unsafe.	
X The classroom arrangement permits student movement with a minimum of disruption.	____ The classroom arrangement inhibits student movement and increases the likelihood of disruption.	
X The classroom arrangement permits the teacher maximum visibility of students.	____ The classroom arrangement limits the teacher's visibility of students.	
X The seating plan maximizes visibility of instructional areas and facilitates student participation.	____ The seating plan limits student visibility of instructional areas and discourages student participation.	Aaron, Paul and Gadhi seated in back of room - talking

Establishing a Climate that Promotes Fairness and Respect (3)

Meets Standards	Does Not Meet Standards	Notes
X The teacher uses student names.	___ The teacher does not use student names.	To Aaron's incorrect response, Mr. I. says "Not hardly."
___ The teacher uses a positive and/or patient vocal tone.	X The teacher uses a negative and/or impatient vocal tone.	When Aaron asked "What's disenfranchise?" Mr. I. answers "Look it up."
___ The teacher applies rules rules consistently and fairly.	X The teacher applies rules inconsistently and unfairly.	Mr. I. ignores Nori's question
___ The teacher encourages student participation and respects student contributions.	X The teacher does not encourage student participation and/or ignores student contributions.	To Paul's correct response he says "see what happens when you pay attention. When Audrey answers "I don't know," Mr. I. says "Why not didn't you read the assignment?"
___ The teacher interacts positively with students and is supportive.	X The teacher ignores or is impatient with students experiencing difficulty.	Matt: "I'm sorry"
___ The teacher provides corrective feedback that preserves student dignity.	X The teacher provides negative/demeaning corrective feedback.	Mr. I.: "You sure are"

Promoting Social Development and Group Responsibility (4)

Meets Standards	Does Not Meet Standards	Notes
___ The teacher conveys an expectation of student attention, cooperation and responsibility.	X The teacher does not convey an expectation of student attention, cooperation and responsibility.	Several students engaged in off-task behaviors (sorting papers, talking, looking around room).
___ Classroom procedures emphasize productive use of time and support student accountability.	X Classroom procedures do not emphasize productive use of time and do not support student accountability.	No response from Mr. I.

Establishing and Maintaining Standards for Student Behavior (5)

Meets Standards	Does Not Meet Standards	Notes
___ Classroom rules and procedures are clearly posted and consistently enforced.	X Classroom rules and procedures are not clearly posted and inconsistently enforced.	Rules posted but not enforced.
___ The teacher monitors student behavior and intervenes when inappropriate or disruptive behavior occurs.	X The teacher does not monitor student behavior and fails to intervene when inappropriate or disruptive behavior occurs.	4 students enter late – no response from Mr. I.
___ The teacher provides specific feedback regarding appropriate/inappropriate student behavior.	X The teacher does not provide specific feedback regarding appropriate/inappropriate student behavior.	No response to off-task behaviors.
___ The teacher uses a variety of verbal and nonverbal signals to stop inappropriate behavior.	X The teacher uses limited/no verbal and nonverbal signals to stop inappropriate behavior.	

Planning and Implementing Classroom Procedures and Routines that Support Student Learning   **(6)**

Meets Standards	Does Not Meet Standards	Notes
____ Activities are structured to maintain appropriate pacing and student engagement.	____ Activities are not structured to maintain appropriate pacing and student engagement.	
X The teacher provides clear instructions for class activities and during transitions between activities.	____ The teacher does not provide clear instructions for class activities and during transitions between activities.	"Get out homework," "put in folder" "take out handout."
____ The teacher identifies and assists those students who do not understand instructions.	X The teacher does not identify and assist those students who do not understand instructions.	Aaron put handout in folder after answering incorrectly.
____ The teacher communicates the value of the lesson's content and activities.	X The teacher fails to communicate the value of the lesson's content and activities.	Test Friday. Most students don't pay attention; few take notes.

Using Instructional Time Effectively   **(7)**

Meets Standards	Does Not Meet Standards	Notes
____ Class begins promptly.	X Class does not begin promptly.	Begins at 8:40
____ Classroom procedures facilitate maximum use of instructional time.	X Classroom procedures do not facilitate maximum use of instructional time.	No procedures in place for students to begin work while teacher attends to routine activities - e.g. attendance
____ The teacher makes full use of instructional time and minimizes interruptions.	X The teacher does not make full use of instructional time and permits frequent interruptions.	

Commentary

(1) In the first section of the instrument Ima records some of the basic information that she will need when she is ready to write her memorandum to Mr. Instructor (e.g., the date, time, and length of the observation, etc.).

(2) This portion of the instrument contains a checklist of statements that reflect classroom environments that do or do not meet standards with respect to "Creating a Physical Environment that Engages All Students." For the most part, the physical arrangement of Bob's classroom meets standards. It is orderly and safe and students are able to move about the classroom and view instructional areas without disruption. Ima's only concern, as her notes reveal, is that Aaron, Paul, and Gadhi's disengagement from the lesson may be the result of a seating plan that places them in the back of the room.

(3) This portion of the instrument relates to "Establishing a Climate that Promotes Fairness and Respect." Bob doesn't fare as well here. While he uses students' names, his tone conveys a negative attitude, he doesn't encourage his students to participate and he is impatient, and in some cases, demeaning, with students experiencing difficulty. Note that Ima records direct quotations from Bob and the students that support the statements she has checked.

(4) This section addresses "Promoting Social Development and Group Responsibility." Bob's classroom practices do not meet this standard's requirements. Bob ignores off-task behavior and does not emphasize the productive use of class time. Again, Ima includes notes that support her observations.

(5) Bob's performance with respect to "Establishing and Maintaining Standards for Student Behavior" is also poor. His classroom rules are clearly posted, but he does not enforce them. He doesn't intervene or redirect students' off-task and disruptive behavior. Ima includes notes about Aaron, Paul and Gadhi's whispering, Jesse and Nari's paper sorting, and Kevin and Jasmine's independent conversation.

(6) Bob doesn't do well with respect to "Planning and Implementing Classroom Procedures and Routines that Support Learning" either. Ima notes that Bob does provide clear instructions between activities. He told students to get out their homework, return it to their folders and to take out their handouts. He does not, however, communicate the value of the lesson beyond the fact that the material will be covered on Friday's test. Bob's lecture appears to be an inappropriate instructional strategy for this group of eighth graders. Most of the students are distracted and only a few take notes during the Ima's observation.

(7) The second standard's requirement to use "Instructional Time Effectively" also is not being met in Bob's classroom. Instruction began ten minutes after the bell had rung and no procedures were in place that permitted students to begin class work while Bob attended to routine classroom procedures (e.g., attendance, attending to the needs of the two students at his desk).

Writing a Focused Observation Memorandum

Ima is now ready to write a memorandum to communicate her observations and her directives to Mr. Instructor.

Surfs Up Unified School District
1234 Sunny Lane
Surfs Up, CA 90000

TO: Mr. Bob Instructor
FROM: Dr. Ima Leader
DATE: September 29, 2003
SUBJECT: Report of Classroom Observation

This memorandum will formally communicate information gathered during my observation of September 23, 2003. I observed from 8:30 to 8:55 while you conducted a lesson on post-Civil War Reconstruction with a group of 24 eighth graders.

During the observation I noted the following teacher and student behaviors with regard to classroom management practices:

1. Four students entered the classroom after the tardy bell. You did not say anything to these students.

2. You began instruction at 8:40 (10 minutes after the beginning of the class period).

3. During the period of my observation, six students took notes. Jesse sorted papers in his notebook and after a time, Nari began to help him. Aaron, Paul, and Gadhi whispered in the back of the room. Kevin and Jasmine held a private conversation by the door. Two students watched me. During this time you continued to lecture and took no action to stop or redirect any of the student behaviors listed.

In addition to the behaviors listed above, I noted several instances in which you exhibited behavior that research has shown to be negatively associated with a supportive learning environment:

1. When Paul was unable to answer correctly, you did not respond to him; you called on another student. Later when Paul answered correctly, you said, "Right, Paul. See what happens when you pay attention?"

2. When Aaron gave an incorrect response, you said, "Not hardly." Later when he asked you what disenfranchise meant, you told him to "look it up."

3. When Audrey told you she did not know the answer, you said, "Why not? Didn't you read the assignment?"

4. When Matt responded to a question with, "I'm sorry, what?" you said, "You sure are" and called on another student.

During this observation, I noted that only Mariana spoke without being called upon. Aaron put away his handout after answering incorrectly. Several students engaged in off-task behaviors (sorting papers, whispering, looking out the window, looking around the room).

The Surfs Up U.S.D. appraisal system has the expectation that you "create and maintain an effective environment for learning." In accomplishing this, it is necessary to: (1) establish and maintain standards for student behavior (2) implement classroom routines or procedures that support learning, and (3) use instructional time effectively.

As part of managing student behavior, the district expects you to (1) interact with students in a fair and equitable manner; (2) communicate and equitably enforce the campus management plan and your own classroom rules, and (3) successfully intervene to stop or redirect off-task and inappropriate behavior. Our district also requires that teachers "establish and maintain a supportive environment." Teacher behaviors that promote a positive learning environment include the following: (1) avoiding sarcasm and negative criticism, (2) exhibiting courtesy and respect, (3) encouraging slow and reluctant students, and (4) maintaining a positive rapport with students.

The data gathered during my observation indicate that these expectations were not met. I will be observing in your classroom again later this month. In all future observations, I expect you to:

1. begin class on time.

2. intervene to redirect off-task student behavior in such a way that all students are engaged in on-task behaviors.

3. positively reinforce or praise student effort and student success in such a way that all students are encouraged to participate.

4. immediately cease all sarcasm and negative criticism in your classroom.

Copy: PAR Council

My signature verifies that I have received a copy of this memorandum. It does not necessarily mean that I agree with the content. I understand that I have the right to present a written response within ten working days.

_____   _____
/s/ Bob Instructor   Date

SUMMARY

In this chapter we have presented a focused observation instrument related to the second CSTP standard, Creating and Maintaining Effective Environments for Student Learning, and demonstrated its use during Bob Instructor's lesson on Reconstruction. The focused observation instrument should be a valuable tool for supervisors, peer coaches, and consulting teachers who wish to gather information on effective classroom environments. In addition, we presented the memorandum Ima Leader drafted after using the instrument. The memorandum clearly communicates what Ima observed and her directives for change. In the following chapter we will expand our discussion to include gathering data and writing documentation related to the third CSTP standard: Understanding and Organizing Subject Matter for Student Learning.

CHAPTER SEVEN: DOCUMENTING CONCERNS ABOUT SUBJECT MATTER PRESENTATION

At the center of the No Child Left Behind (NCLB) Act is the requirement that teachers of core subject matter areas be "highly qualified." Under accompanying federal regulations, elementary teachers are deemed highly qualified if, among other things, they are state certified, have a bachelor's degree, and demonstrate subject matter knowledge in reading/ language arts, writing, mathematics and other areas of the elementary curriculum. If the teacher is new to the profession, the teacher must have passed a rigorous state test. If the teacher is not new to the profession, the teacher must either pass such a test or demonstrate competency through systematic evaluations. Middle and secondary school teachers must be similarly state-certified and hold a bachelor's degree. If the teacher is new to the profession, the teacher must have a college degree in the subject being taught or its equivalent, have advanced credentialing, or pass a rigorous state test in the subject area the teacher teaches. If not new to the profession, the teacher can establish competency in this manner or through systematic evaluations (34 C.F.R. § 200.56).

UNDERSTANDING AND ORGANIZING SUBJECT MATTER

The NCLB's emphasis on content knowledge in combination with systematic evaluations to document it has direct relevance to the third standard of the California Standards for the Teaching Profession (CSTP), Understanding and Organizing Subject Matter for Student Learning. The third standard outlines California's requirements for teachers' understanding of subject matter and their ability to organize this knowledge for student learning. In addressing subject area content, the third standard highlights the need for teachers to make connections between subject areas and integrate appropriate materials and technology into the lesson.

The table (Figure 7-1 on the next page) outlines the research supporting each component of the third standard organized in terms of student and teacher behaviors. A bibliography of this research is included as Appendix E.

The focus on teacher content knowledge requires that evaluators pay attention to teachers' understanding of their subject matter and how they organize and present information to students. Teachers must have strong communication skills. Effective teachers are able to communicate the lesson's goals and objectives, present examples, explain di-

Figure 7-1

Standard Three

UNDERSTANDING AND ORGANIZING SUBJECT MATTER FOR STUDENT LEARNING

3-1 DEMONSTRATING KNOWLEDGE OF SUBJECT MATTER CONTENT AND STUDENT DEVELOPMENT

The teacher:
- presents current content and/or skills.
- is logical and clear in the presentation and explanation of content.
- incorporates relevant examples, step-by-step explanations and clear demonstrations of how to do work.
- allows time for student thinking after explanation and for student practice.
- understands students' cognitive, social and emotional development.

Students:
- work at the appropriate cognitive and linguistic level.
- are able to practice the lesson's concepts and skills.
- are encouraged to interact at appropriate social, emotional and physical levels of development.

3-2 ORGANIZING CURRICULUM TO SUPPORT STUDENT UNDERSTANDING OF SUBJECT MATTER

The teacher:
- aligns course objectives, instruction and assessment.
- organizes the lesson to present key concepts and themes.
- maintains pacing and student engagement through careful structuring of activities.
- uses proactive expression and repetition to facilitate instruction.
- incorporates materials that are appropriate to the students' development, interests and needs.
- incorporates higher level cognitive questions.
- varies the pace of instruction to accommodate students' ability levels.

Students:
- are able to recognize and apply key concepts and themes.
- are engaged with the lesson.
- are able to understand and apply the lesson's examples and materials.
- are engaged in problem solving and application activities.
- are able to work at the appropriate developmental level.

3-3 INTERRELATING IDEAS AND INFORMATION WITHIN AND ACROSS SUBJECT MATTER AREAS

The teacher:
- emphasizes the connections between subject areas when presenting content.
- integrates cross-curricular themes and concepts.
- makes connections between the lesson's content and students' interests and home environments.

Students:
- recognize connections between subject areas.
- apply problem solving techniques from other disciplines when appropriate.
- make connections between the lesson's content and their own interests and/or home environments.

3-4 DEVELOPING STUDENT UNDERSTANDING THROUGH INSTRUCTIONAL STRATEGIES THAT ARE APPROPRIATE TO THE SUBJECT MATTER

The teacher:
- provides for active participation by students.
- conducts frequent controlled group practice over new material.
- asks questions that require students to apply, analyze, synthesize, and evaluate information.
- emphasizes higher mental processes in instruction.
- uses a variety of instructional strategies and approaches when presenting subject content.
- assists students in constructing their own knowledge of subject matter.

Students:
- are actively engaged in the lesson.
- engage in higher level thinking and application activities.
- are able to construct their own meaning in the lesson.

3-5 USING MATERIALS, RESOURCES AND TECHNOLOGIES TO MAKE SUBJECT MATTER MORE ACCESSIBLE TO STUDENTS

The teacher:
- uses materials that are appropriate to the students' interests, experiences, and needs.
- integrates technology into the lesson when appropriate.
- incorporates materials and resources reflective of the classroom's diversity.

Students:
- are able to understand and use the lesson's materials.
- use technology to appropriately access materials resources.

rections, and provide feedback in clear terms. Their written class materials (e.g., handouts, board work, transparencies, etc.) utilize correct grammar, spelling, and usage, and these teachers use language that is appropriate for the developmental level of their students. In addition, teachers need to implement instructional strategies that are appropriate to both the subject matter and students' abilities. Instructional strategies should support student understanding of the subject and facilitate connections between subject areas.

Using a Focused Observation Instrument to Gather and Record Data

Suppose Ima Leader has concerns that Bob Instructor is presenting information that is developmentally inappropriate for students and that his organization of instruction is ineffective. Ima has heard students complain that his content is too hard and that his instruction is generally disorganized. With this in mind, Ima plans to observe Bob's classroom using the focused observation instrument tailored to the third CSTP standard. This enables her to focus her data gathering on those attributes of the lesson that relate specifically to Bob's knowledge of his subject and his presentation of information.

Some of the data Ima gathers about Bob's subject matter knowledge will come from his written materials. Ima asks for copies of course handouts and checks Bob's board work and overhead transparencies for the accuracy of information presented, grammar, spelling and usage. Ima feels comfortable assessing Bob's content on Reconstruction because she was a history major in college and taught high school history for five years before moving into administration. When Ima is not as knowledgeable about a teacher's subject, she sometimes asks a subject area department head familiar with the content to conduct this type of observation. Peer coaches and consulting teachers will find this instrument to be a useful tool in helping the teachers they mentor to identify weaknesses in their subject matter presentation and supporting their improvement.

On entering Bob's class Ima collects a copy of the handout that Bob assigned for the previous night's reading assignment. The handout is a copy of a short section of a chapter on Civil War Reconstruction in the South. The copied text appears to be that of an upper level high school course, and its vocabulary and treatment of the subject matter are considerably more sophisticated than what Ima expects Bob's students can comfortably master.

What follows is Ima's completed focused observation from Mr. Instructor's class on Reconstruction (see "script" in Chapter 5). A blank copy of this instrument is included in Appendix A. Note that the numbers on the form correspond with appropriate discussions in the commentary section that follows.

FOCUSED OBSERVATION INSTRUMENT #3

Understanding and Organizing Subject Matter for Student Learning

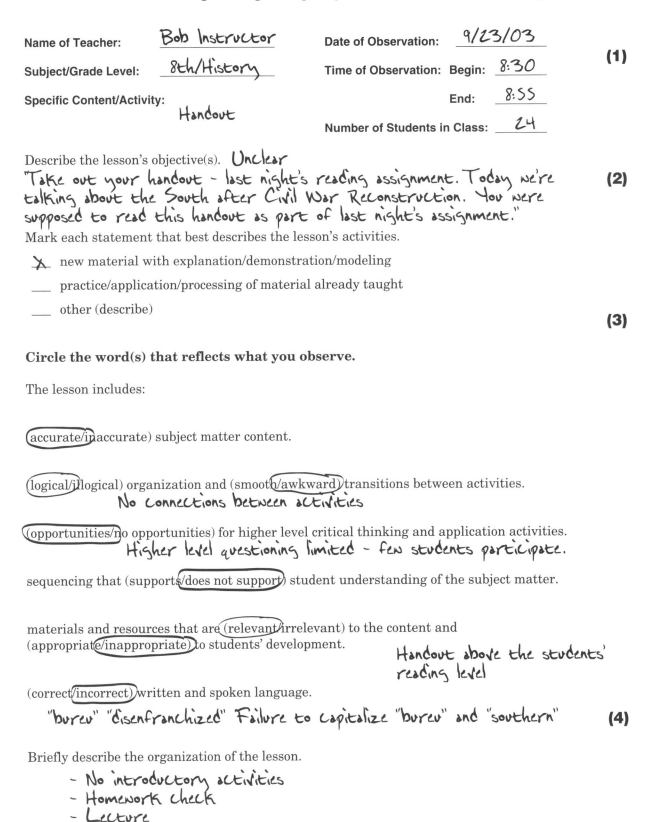

Name of Teacher: Bob Instructor   Date of Observation: 9/23/03

(1)

Subject/Grade Level: 8th/History   Time of Observation: Begin: 8:30

Specific Content/Activity: End: 8:55

Handout

Number of Students in Class: 24

Describe the lesson's objective(s). Unclear

"Take out your handout - last night's reading assignment. Today we're talking about the South after Civil War Reconstruction. You were supposed to read this handout as part of last night's assignment."

(2)

Mark each statement that best describes the lesson's activities.

X   new material with explanation/demonstration/modeling

___   practice/application/processing of material already taught

___   other (describe)

(3)

Circle the word(s) that reflects what you observe.

The lesson includes:

(accurate/inaccurate) subject matter content.

(logical/illogical) organization and (smooth/awkward) transitions between activities.
No connections between activities

(opportunities/no opportunities) for higher level critical thinking and application activities.
Higher level questioning limited - few students participate.

sequencing that (supports/does not support) student understanding of the subject matter.

materials and resources that are (relevant/irrelevant) to the content and
(appropriate/inappropriate) to students' development.
Handout above the students' reading level

(correct/incorrect) written and spoken language.
"bureu" "disenfranchized" Failure to capitalize "bureu" and "southern"

(4)

Briefly describe the organization of the lesson.
- No introductory activities
- Homework check
- Lecture

Briefly describe the lesson's activities and their sequence.

- check homework
- lecture / questions

(5)

What strategies does the teacher utilize to move students from the knowledge/comprehension to application of the skill or concept taught?

X higher level questioning   ___ performance/demonstration

___ group work   ___ independent products

___ paper/pencil activity   ___ other (describe)

     10 questions to 4 students

Describe evidence that students are successful/(unsuccessful) in reaching the lesson's objectives.

- Few read assignment
- Difficulty with vocabulary
- Themes/concepts unclear

(6)

Do students make connections between the current instruction and

___ prior learning?   ___ students' lives and experiences?

___ other subject areas?   ___ issues beyond the classroom?

     No connections made

How does the teacher provide for students to make connections?

___ The teacher tells/explains the connection.

___ The teacher facilitates a process (discussion, activity, etc.) through which students recognize connections.

     No connections made

(7)

List/describe the materials, resources and technologies incorporated into the lesson?

     Handout

Summary of Data and Evaluation of Understanding and Organizing Subject Matter for Student Learning **(8)**

The statements on the left reflect classroom instruction that has effectively organized subject matter and content for student understanding and learning. These statements reflect classrooms that meet the requirements of third CSTP standard. The statements on the right reflect classroom instruction that do not meet standards. Include notes that detail and/or support your observations. The number(s) in parentheses indicate the component(s) of the third standard that is or is not being met.

Meets Standards	Does Not Meet Standards	Notes
____ The focus of instruction is clear (3-1; 3-2).	X The focus of instruction is unclear (3-1; 3-2).	Objective not clearly stated.
X Instructional content and/or skills are relevant and new (3-1).	____ Instructional content and/or skills are repetitive and/or irrelevant (3-1).	
____ The presentation of the subject matter is logical and clear (3-2).	X The presentation of the subject matter is not logical or unclear (3-2).	New material on Reconstruction.
X Learning is organized around the central themes/ concepts of the discipline (3-1; 3-3).	____ Learning is not organized around the central themes/ concepts of the discipline; learning is miscellaneous and unconnected (3-1; 3-3).	
____ The critical attributes of the concept or skill being taught are elaborated in ways that lead to student mastery (3-1; 3-2; 3-3).	X The critical attributes of the concept or skill being taught are unclear and students are unsuccessful (3-1; 3-2; 3-3).	Few students understand concepts
____ The teacher incorporates relevant examples, explanations and/or demonstrations of the subject matter (3-3; 3-4; 3-5).	X The teacher does not incorporate relevant examples, explanations and/or demonstrations of the subject matter (3-3; 3-4; 3-5).	No examples, explanations or demonstrations
____ The teacher repeats information and responds appropriately to student questions (3-2).	X The teacher does not repeat information and does not respond appropriately to student questions (3-2).	Ignores Nori's question when Aaron asks "What's disenfranchise?" Mr. I. responds "Look it up"
____ The teacher teaches, reteaches and reviews as necessary (3-2).	X The teacher does not teach, reteach and review as necessary (3-2).	Limited questioning
X Students have opportunities to engage in critical thinking, problem solving and/or creative inquiry (3-3; 3-4).	____ Students do not have opportunities to engage in critical thinking, problem solving and/or creative inquiry (3-3; 3-4).	

____ Students have opportunities to connect/ apply learning to other disciplines, their own lives, and issues beyond the classroom (3-3; 3-4).

__X__ Students do not have opportunities to connect/ apply learning to other disciplines, their own lives, and issues beyond the classroom (3-3; 3-4).

No connections made

____ Students' active engagement and participation indicate that the lesson's content and activities are interesting (3-2; 3-5).

__X__ Students' lack of active engagement and participation indicate the the lesson's content and activities are not interesting (3-2; 3-5).

Most students do not pay attention, few take notes

____ Content and instructional strategies represent the current/best practice within the subject area (3-1; 3-4).

__X__ Content and instructional strategies do not represent the current/best practice within the subject area (3-1; 3-4).

____ Instructional materials relate to the subject matter and are relevant to students' interests and needs (3-2; 3-5).

__X__ Instructional materials do not relate to the subject matter and/or are not relevant to students' interests and needs (3-2; 3-5).

Reading level of handout above that of students.

____ Relevant technology is incorporated, when appropriate, in the lesson (3-5).

____ Relevant and appropriate use of technology is omitted from the lesson (3-5).

____ The course objectives, instruction and assessment are aligned (3-1; 3-4).

____ The course objectives, instruction and assessment are not aligned (3-1; 3-4).

Commentary

(1) The first section of the instrument provides essential information that Ima will need when she is ready to write her memorandum to Mr. Instructor (e.g., date, time, and length of observation, etc.)

(2) In this section, Ima records the exact words Bob used to begin the lesson. Ima notes that the introduction did not contain a statement of the learning outcome or objective. Below is a space for Ima to record the type of lesson she is observing. She marks that Mr. Instructor is introducing new material.

(3) Here Ima circles the words that reflect what she observes. She records notes that support her observations to the right of the statements. She marks that Bob presents accurate information. His organization is logical but his transitions are awkward. He does not connect the content of the current lecture to prior learning or the homework. Bob's questions provide some opportunity for students to engage in higher level activities, but Ima notes that this opportunity is rather limited. Ima does not feel that the sequence of activities supports student learning. She notes that while the materials are relevant to the lesson, the handout is too sophisticated for the eighth graders Bob is teaching. Finally, Ima notes that Bob's lesson contained inaccurate use of language. She records the exact language from Bob's board work. While we strongly advocate avoiding judgments during the data collection process, some instructional issues (e.g., smooth/awkward transitions) may be appropriate if accompanied by the objective data that led to the judgment. In those cases, Ima noted "No connections between activities" – the objective evidence that led to her judgment.

(4) In this section, Ima briefly describes the organization of the lesson as well as the sequence of activities.

(5) Here Ima notes that the only strategy Bob utilized to move students toward application of the lesson's concepts was questioning. Her evidence indicates the students were not successful. Bob asked ten questions to four students, but only two students were able to answer correctly. She also notes that students appeared to have difficulty with the handout's vocabulary and that the lesson's themes were unclear.

(6) This section contains indicators of the third standard's requirement of connecting content to other subject areas. Ima indicates that neither Bob nor his students made any connections to other subjects or to interests outside of the classroom.

(7) This section asks for a list of materials, resources and technologies used in instruction. The only resource included in Bob's lesson is the copied handout.

(8) Ima completes this summary data section after the observation is over. Here she summarizes what she observed during Bob's lesson. The headings "Meets Standards" and "Does Not Meet Standards" allow her to evaluate Bob's performance with respect to the individual components of the third standard.

Writing a Focused Observation Memorandum

Ima is now ready to write the focused observation memorandum that addresses Bob's understanding and organizing subject matter for student learning.

Surfs Up Unified School District
1234 Sunny Lane
Surfs Up, CA 90000

TO: Mr. Bob Instructor
FROM: Dr. Ima Leader
DATE: September 29, 2003
SUBJECT: Report of Classroom Observation

This memorandum will formally communicate information gathered during my observation of September 23, 2003. I observed from 8:30 to 8:55 while you conducted a lesson on post-Civil War Reconstruction with a group of 24 eighth graders.

The observation revealed the following information:

1. You began by saying, "Take out your handout—last night's reading assignment. Today we're going to be talking about the South after the Civil War, Reconstruction. You were supposed to read this handout as part of last night's assignment." There was no communication of the specific learning outcome/objective.

2. While it was clear that you know this period of American history well, the lesson's content consisted of miscellaneous and unconnected information. You did not link the content of instruction to the homework or to previous learning. The discussion was disconnected (e.g., vocabulary words, facts about Reconstruction, etc.) and you did not relate the content to other subject areas or to students' interests or experiences.

3. You asked ten higher-level questions (i.e., at the application level or higher on Bloom's Taxonomy) to four different students. Two of these students (Mariana and Paul) were successful.

4. While your spoken English was correct, your written English contained several errors. When listing the significant achievements of the Freedman's Bureau, you misspelled two words ("disenfranchized" and "bureu") and failed to capitalize "bureu' and "southern" in one instance.

5. The reading level of the handout was well above that of your students. Several students (Nari and Aaron) were struggling with the vocabulary used and Paul did not grasp the concept of Reconstruction. The students' apparent failure to read the assignment also suggested that the reading might be too difficult.

The Surfs Up U.S.D. appraisal system has the expectation that you organize and present subject matter for student learning. Within that evaluation standard, there is an expectation that you communicate learning objectives and organize activities in such a way that students are able to achieve these objectives. This requires that you implement strategies that move students toward higher level thinking skills and that you make connections to other subject areas and/or to issues beyond the classroom. In addition, there is an expectation that you incorporate materials and resources that are appropriate to students' developmental levels and use spoken as well as written language correctly.

The data from my observation indicate that these expectations related to the third CSTP standard are not being met. Please contact your eighth grade team leader to explore how you might tailor your teaching materials to the age level of your students. If you have questions or concerns about communicating learning objectives, implementing application level activities or making connections between subject areas, please contact the PAR consulting teacher for the social studies department, Ms. Lenda Hand.

I will be observing in your classroom again beginning two weeks from today. In all future observations I will expect to observe you meeting the district's expectations for organizing and presenting subject matter for student learning as listed above.

Copy: PAR Council

Ms. Lenda Hand

My signature verifies that I have received a copy of this memorandum. It does not necessarily mean that I agree with the content. I understand that I have the right to present a written response within ten working days.

_____   _____
/s/ Bob Instructor   Date

SUMMARY

In this chapter we have introduced and demonstrated the use of a focused observation instrument tailored to the third CSTP standard. The focused observation instrument was accompanied by a memorandum that summarized the data from the observation and set forth expectations for future teacher and student behavior related to classroom management and environment. A supervisor might use the instrument to document unsatisfactory classroom performance and may write memoranda to notify Mr. Instructor of his deficiencies or document his non-compliance with a professional growth plan. It is unlikely that peer coaches or consulting teachers would write such memoranda, but we believe the focused observation instrument will ease their responsibilities when observing teachers and sharing information, either in conferences with the teacher or in reporting to the district/school level PAR committee. In the following chapter, we will expand our discussion to include gathering data and writing documentation related to Standard Four: Planning Instruction and Designing Learning Experiences for All Students.

CHAPTER EIGHT: DOCUMENTING INSTRUCTIONAL PLANNING

Effective planning is an integral component of good teaching. Students learn best when instructional plans link current content to previous learning and to their own backgrounds and interests. In planning instruction, effective teachers establish clear learning objectives and sequence the curriculum in order to maximize student achievement of these goals. This means developing long- and short-term plans that facilitate student understanding of the subject matter. Effective teachers plan instructional activities that promote student learning and encourage connections between other subject areas as well as to students' lives and experiences. When students are unengaged in the learning or demonstrate poor performance, effective teachers revise their instructional plans and modify strategies to better fit students' characteristics and abilities.

Without knowledge of lesson planning, an evaluator may misjudge a teacher's classroom behavior. The rationale for learning objectives, instructional strategies, curriculum materials, and assessment strategies may not be immediately apparent during a classroom observation. Thus, depending on the terms of collective bargaining agreement, evaluators may want to consider the teacher's lesson plans when assessing instruction. A teacher's planning strategies can be determined either in discussions with the teacher or through an assessment of the teacher's written lesson plans.

In this chapter we will address gathering information from an examination of a teacher's written lesson plan. In the previous three chapters, we addressed gathering data from direct classroom observation. This chapter differs in that it is concerned with collecting information from the written lesson plans and not from observing classroom behaviors. This is not to say that evidence of effective planning is not evident during a classroom observation, only that consideration of a teacher's lesson plans enables evaluators to understand the intent of instruction and how well the teacher's classroom behaviors and practices corresponded to what was planned.

PLANNING INSTRUCTION AND DESIGNING LEARNING EXPERIENCES

We use the fourth standard of the California Standards for the Teaching Profession (CSTP): Planning Instruction and Designing Learning Experiences for All Students as our guide in assessing the effectiveness of lesson planning. This standard encompasses issues related to clearly identifying learning goals, sequencing subject matter content and activities for student learning, and modifying instruction to accommodate students' backgrounds and needs.

As we previously have noted, the instruments we present in this handbook are based on the current and best research on effective teaching. A bibliography of the supporting research these instruments can be found in Appendix E. The table (Figure 8-1 on the next page) presents the research related to each element of the fourth standard in terms of teacher and student behaviors.

Figure 8-1

Standard Four
PLANNING INSTRUCTION AND DESIGNING LEARNING EXPERIENCES FOR ALL STUDENTS

4-1 DRAWING ON AND VALUING STUDENT'S BACKGROUNDS, INTERESTS, AND DEVELOPMENTAL NEEDS

The teacher:
- plans instruction and activities that relate to students' lives, experiences, and interests.
- uses materials that are appropriate to students' interests, needs, and developmental levels.
- plans instruction to recognize and accommodate student diversity.

Students:
- are motivated and engage in on-task behaviors.
- actively participate in the lesson.
- initiate their own learning.

4-2 ESTABLISHING AND ARTICULATING GOALS

The teacher:
- clearly communicates the goals of the lesson.
- plans activities that are related to the lesson's goals.
- secures student attention before proceeding with the lesson.
- explains the purpose of the lesson and questions to determine student understanding when providing instructions.
- emphasizes the value of instruction.

Students:
- understand the lesson's purpose.
- understand directions and are able to participate in the lesson's activities.

4-3 DEVELOPING AND SEQUENCING INSTRUCTIONAL ACTIVITIES AND MATERIALS FOR STUDENT LEARNING

The teacher:
- sequences and paces instruction to maximize student understanding and engagement.
- sequences activities to promote critical thinking.
- plans activities appropriate to the lesson's complexity.
- asks frequent questions.
- allows appropriate wait time for student responses.
- uses detail and redundancy when presenting the lesson.

Students:
- are engaged in critical thinking activities.
- remain engaged in the lesson's activities.
- are able to successfully respond to questions.

4-4 DESIGNING SHORT-TERM AND LONG-TERM PLANS TO FOSTER STUDENT LEARNING

The teacher:
- develops short and long term plans for instruction.
- conducts regular assessments of student learning.
- incorporates formal and informal assessments.
- revises plans contingent upon results of assessments.

Students:
- are able to keep up with the pace of instruction.
- understand the results of assessments.

4-5 MODIFYING INSTRUCTIONAL PLANS TO ADJUST FOR STUDENT NEEDS

The teacher:
- matches the pace of instruction to the needs of students.
- modifies plans to accommodate students of varying ability levels.
- identifies low-achieving students, monitors their performance, and implements instructional recommendations.
- modifies the cognitive level of questions according to the ability level of students.
- provides frequent and graphic performance feedback to students.
- allows for frequent individualized interactions with students.

Students:
- have frequent opportunities for individual interaction with the teacher.
- are able to participate with a high degree of success.
- remain interested in the lesson.

Using a Focused Observation Instrument to Gather and Record Data

You may recall from Chapter 5 that Ima Leader planned to refer Bob Instructor for Peer Assistance and Review (PAR) support. In this chapter we find Bob working with his consulting teacher, Ms. Lenda Hand. The PAR committee believes that poor planning strategies may be at the root of Bob's ineffective teaching behavior and has asked Lenda to support Bob in making changes in this area of his teaching practice.

Lenda is well aware of the importance of careful planning to effective teaching and student learning. As a skilled veteran teacher, she understands that each group of students and each school year are different. For Lenda, this is part of the joy of teaching—no two groups of students and no two class periods or school years are ever quite the same. While she enjoys the diversity of teaching, she realizes the challenges it poses and the demands it places on teachers. She knows that effective teaching requires that teachers regularly reassess their approach to lesson design and that effective instructional planning requires that teachers reflect on students' classroom performances and modify instruction to meet students' needs.

Although Lenda is able to identify some key areas of weakness on her first reading of Bob's lesson plans, she knows that her conference with Bob and her report to the PAR committee will be more effective if she can support her evaluation with objective evidence of Bob's strengths and weaknesses. To help her in this task, she chooses the instrument tailored to the fourth standard of the CSTP. Lenda checks the boxes that reflect what she finds as she examines Bob written lesson plan and takes notes that support her findings. Bob's lesson plan (Figure 8-2) is on the next page.

What follows is Lenda's completed focused evaluation instrument from her examination of Mr. Instructor's lesson plan for the week of September 22. A blank copy of this instrument is included in Appendix A. Notice that there are numbers in parentheses in each section of the form. These numbers correspond with the comments in the commentary that follows.

Figure 8-2   WEEKLY LESSON PLAN – SURFS UP UNIFIED SCHOOL DISTRICT

Name: Bob Instructor		Week of: September 22		State/District Learning Standards: 8.11 – The Consequences of Reconstruction (1) aims and effects, (2) experiences of former slaves, (3) effects of Freedmen's Bureau, etc.	
Subject: U.S. History		Grade/Class Period(s): 8th Grade/1st Period			
	Monday	Tuesday	Wednesday	Thursday	Friday
Objectives for Learning	Vocabulary Geography	Understanding Reconstruction	Understanding Reconstruction (cont.)	Understanding Reconstruction (cont.) Vocabulary	Understanding Reconstruction (cont.)
Instructional Strategies	• Students look up voc. words (quiz Thurs.) • Use each word in a written sentence – (keep in folders) • Students color maps to identify different regions of the U.S. during Reconstruction (keep in folders)	• Check homework • Lecture/ Discussion related to homework reading • Students answer questions/take notes • In class reading – Chapter Six (pp. 187-201)	• Collect paragraphs • Watch video – "Buffalo Soldiers"	• Vocabulary quiz • Lecture: "Jim Crow," the 14th Amendment and Radical Reconstruction • Students take notes on outline (keep in folder) • Answer questions/ review for test	Test over Reconstruction
Materials/Resources	Dictionaries Maps (blank)	Text	Buffalo Soldiers video	Handout: Lecture outline	NA
Accommodations for Student Needs			Video – most students don't read well		
Homework/Assessment	HW: Read Handout – "Rebuilding the South" Answer questions 4, 6 & 8	HW: Write a paragraph explaining how Blacks responded to emancipation	HW: Study for vocabulary quiz	Vocabulary quiz HW: Study for test	Test

FOCUSED OBSERVATION INSTRUMENT #4

Planning Instruction and Designing Learning Experiences for All Students

Name of Teacher: Bob Instructor   **Date(s) of Review:** 9/22-9/26/03

Subject/Grade Level: 8th/History   **Number of Students:** 24   **(1)**

Course Content or Unit of Study: Civil War Reconstruction

Review the lesson plans for dates cited above and check the statements that best describe your observations. The number(s) in parentheses indicate the component(s) of the fourth standard that is or is not being met.

Meets Standards	Does Not Meet Standards	Notes **(2)**
X Lesson plans are completed in accordance with district policies and campus level requirments.	____ Lesson plans are not completed in accordance with district policies and campus level requirments.	
____ Learning objectives are clearly stated (4-2).	X Learning objectives are unclear (4-2).	States topic/subject but not objective
X Lesson plans outline the presentation of relevant and new content and/or skills (4-3).	____ Lesson plans do not outline the presentation of relevant and new content and/or skills (4-3).	New material on Reconstruction.
X Lesson content is organized around the central themes/ concepts of the discipline (4-3).	____ Lesson content is not organized around the central themes/ concepts of the discipline (4-3).	
____ Lesson plans include activities that allow students to engage in critical thinking, problem solving and/or creative inquiry (4-3).	X Lesson plans do not include activities that allow students to engage in critical thinking, problem solving and/or creative inquiry (4-3).	No opportunities for higher-level application activities. All activities require passive student participation.
____ The lesson(s)' activities are appropriate for students' developmental level and abilities (4-1).	X The lesson(s)' activities are inappropriate for students' developmental level and abilities (4-1).	Students need more "student-centered" learning where students complete projects, etc.
____ Lesson plans include activities and materials that are related to students' interests and needs (4-1).	X Lesson plans do not include activities and materials that are related to students' interests and needs (4-1).	No connection to student interests
____ Lesson plans include activities that allow students to connect/apply learning to other disciplines, their own lives and issues beyond the classroom (4-1).	X Lesson plans do not include activities that allow students to connect/apply learning to other disciplines, their own lives and issues beyond the classroom (4-1).	Most activities teacher-directed no connections to other subject areas
____ The lesson's activities are differentiated for students of varying abilities. (4-5).	X The lesson's activities are not differentiated for students of varying abilities. (4-5).	No evidence of differentiated instruction
____ The lesson plans show evidence of short and long term planning (4-4).	X The lesson plans do not show evidence of short and long term planning (4-4).	
____ The lesson plans reflect accommodations for students' individual needs (4-5).	X The lesson plans do not reflect accommodations for students' individual needs (4-5).	Showing video not really an accommodation for poor readers.

Commentary

(1) In the first section of the instrument, Lenda records some of the basic information that she will need in her communications with Mr. Instructor, Ima and/or the PAR committee (e.g., the date of the review, name of the teacher, subject/grade level, etc.).

(2) This portion of the instrument contains a checklist of statements reflecting lesson plans that do or do not meet the requirements of the fourth CSTP standard. As Lenda's notes indicate, she has concerns that Bob may not be clearly expressing learning objectives and that his instructional strategies do not include activities that allow students to think creatively about the subject matter or to make connections with their own lives and/or other subject areas. She also has concerns that Bob's instructional format of lecture, note taking and discussion does not permit students to become actively engaged with the subject matter. His lesson plan does not provide opportunities for students to apply their learning or make connections to other areas of their lives. The activities he has planned require that students interact with the material in a passive manner (e.g., looking up words, writing sentences, reading from the text, watching a video, listening to a lecture). Finally, she notes that showing a video doesn't necessarily accommodate students' individual needs.

Lenda's Conference with Bob

When Lenda meets with Bob she brings a copy of her completed instrument and shares the information that she has collected. Including the instrument in the conference helps her to communicate her findings in an objective format and reduces the possibility that Bob will dismiss her suggestions as matters of opinion or instructional bias.

She opens by complimenting Bob on the completeness of his plans. Each component of the plan is filled out. She notes that this not always the case and that it is much easier to work with teachers who understand the district's lesson plan requirements.

In the discussion that follows she shares her concerns that Bob is not clearly establishing learning objectives and that his instructional strategies do not permit students to engage with the subject matter in meaningful ways. This surprises Bob. He explains that he thought the objectives were pretty clear and that his lecture format was a good way to convey a great deal of information about Reconstruction in a short time. Lenda asks Bob if his students know what they will do with this information or if they know how it connects to other subject areas or their own experiences. Bob confides that he has noticed his students often seem confused by and disinterested in the subject matter and that they generally don't do very well on his tests.

Lenda suggests that perhaps students aren't recognizing the purpose or value of the lesson. Bob nods and explains that this group of students doesn't appreciate history or see its relevance. Lenda responds that perhaps part of the problem is that they don't understand what it is they are supposed to know about Reconstruction. On Bob's lesson plan the objectives aren't clear. He has written the subject that will be covered, but he hasn't said what students will be able to understand or do with the information he presents or how they will demonstrate their learning. Lenda has brought a copy of a workshop handout on writing clear learning objectives for Bob, and she suggests that he might want to attend the workshop when it is offered again in November.

Lenda next points out that Bob's lesson plans rely heavily on seatwork and passive learning. She explains that Bob's students probably need more active, learner–centered activities. His students need to analyze, solve problems and apply the concepts they study in order to fully engage with the learning. They also need to see the connections between what they learn and their own lives.

Bob looks skeptical. "I've taught history for a long time," he says. "My methods used to work quite well, but these new groups of students don't read. I accommodate them— I show more videos, but I still don't think they get it." Lenda laughs and agrees that the students have changed but asserts that teachers need to change too. She suggests that Bob incorporate more activities where students create products that demonstrate their learning. He might want to organize students into groups to complete projects about the historical periods they study. She explains that she has had success when she allows students to take on the roles of people they study about. In her Reconstruction unit, she assigns students to "become" scalawags, carpetbaggers, emancipated blacks, Buffalo Soldiers, Radical Republicans, Southern farmers, and even President Johnson. Once in character, the students must explain their positions and debate the merits of their points of view. "The students get very excited about it," she explains, "and they teach one another when they debate. Most students even try to dress in character when they know they must present."

Bob admits that it's a great idea, and Lenda suggests several publications and web sites that publish innovative lesson plans for active learning in history and the social sciences. Bob thanks Lenda for the ideas and says that he'll work to be clearer about objectives and to plan more learner-centered activities in the future.

Lenda writes a brief summary of her meeting with Bob. She sends a copy to the PAR committee with the completed lesson plan instrument attached.

SUMMARY

In this chapter we have presented a focused data collection instrument related to the fourth CSTP standard, Planning Instruction and Designing Learning Experiences for All Students, and demonstrated its use for Bob Instructor's written lesson plan on Reconstruction. The focused data collection instrument should be a valuable tool for supervisors, peer coaches, and consulting teachers who wish to gather information on lesson planning.

It is worthwhile to note that while this instrument may be used to evaluate written plans alone, it may also be used to supplement the classroom observation instruments presented in the other chapters of this handbook. Effective lesson planning is best realized in the classroom environment, and supervisors and consulting teachers may want to compare what is written on plans to what occurs in the classroom in order to fully assess the effects of planning. In the following chapter, we will expand our discussion to include gathering data and writing documentation related to the fifth CSTP standard, Assessing Student Learning.

CHAPTER NINE: DOCUMENTING THE ASSESSMENT OF STUDENT LEARNING

In this chapter we will address gathering information and documenting instruction with respect to the fifth standard of the California Standards for the Teaching Profession (CSTP): Assessing Student Learning. This standard encompasses issues related to establishing goals for learning, assessing student learning and guiding students in assessing their own learning, using the results of assessment to guide instruction, and communicating with parents and others about student progress.

The table (Figure 9-1 on the next page) outlines the supporting research related to each component the fifth standard organized in terms of student and teacher behaviors. A bibliography of this research is included as Appendix E.

ASSESSMENT OF STUDENT LEARNING

Assessment of student learning is an essential tool of good teaching. Effective teachers provide frequent opportunities for students to demonstrate and apply their learning. Assessments may be informal or formal. Teachers informally assess students' understanding when they ask questions or ask students to provide summaries, demonstrations, definitions or examples. Graded work generally represents more formal assessment. Teachers must respond to both types of assessment in a timely and appropriate manner. When speaking to students, teachers should provide encouraging corrective feedback when students are having difficulty and positive reinforcement when they are successful. Students should understand the standards for graded assignments and should be held accountable for their work.

Using a Focused Observation Instrument to Gather and Record Data

Suppose that Principal Ima Leader now has concerns that Mr. Instructor is not assessing student learning appropriately. She is concerned that the lecture-discussion format that Bob favors provides little opportunity for assessment, and when it does, Bob often provides inappropriate feedback.

Ima plans a classroom observation in which she will focus her data collection on these issues. To help her in this task, she chooses the focused observation instrument tailored to the fifth standard of the CSTP. Readers will note that this instrument is very similar to the focused observation instrument for the first CSTP standard, Engaging and Supporting All Students in Learning.

What follows is Ima's completed focused observation instrument from Mr. Instructor's class on Reconstruction (see Chapter 5's "script" of the lesson). A blank copy of this instrument is included in Appendix A. The numbers on the form correspond with the notes that follow in the commentary section of this discussion.

Figure 9-1

Standard Five
ASSESSING STUDENT LEARNING

5-1 ESTABLISHING AND COMMUNICATING LEARNING GOALS FOR ALL STUDENTS

The teacher:
- clearly communicates the lesson's objectives.
- presents a clear rationale for the lesson.
- aligns learning goals with subject matter concepts and skills.
- aligns learning goals with course assessments.
- aligns learning goals with students' developmental levels.

Students:
- demonstrate a clear understanding of lesson objectives.
- understand instructions and are able to successfully complete activities.
- are able to work at the appropriate developmental level.

5-2 COLLECTING AND USING MULTIPLE SOURCES OF INFORMATION TO ASSESS STUDENT LEARNING

The teacher:
- carefully monitors students' academic progress.
- uses a variety of assessment strategies.
- uses performance assessments that allow students to demonstrate their understanding of content in meaningful ways.
- incorporates frequent assessments of student mastery and provides frequent feedback to students.

Students:
- have opportunities to demonstrate their learning in a variety of formats.
- are aware of their academic progress.

5-3 INVOLVING AND GUIDING ALL STUDENTS IN ASSESSING THEIR OWN LEARNING

The teacher:
- integrates assessment into the learning process.
- holds students accountable for reasonable standards of work.
- provides opportunities for student to monitor themselves.
- monitors student responses in order to ascertain student understanding and success.
- models strategies for assessment.

Students:
- understand the learning goals and are able to monitor their progress.
- utilize self-assessment strategies.

5-4 USING THE RESULTS OF ASSESSMENTS TO GUIDE INSTRUCTION

The teacher:
- aligns course objectives, instruction and assessment and provides feedback and correction when needed.
- uses assessment results to guide instructional planning.
- provided the necessary corrective strategies following instruction and testing.
- uses assessment results to guide individual student learning.

Students:
- Not applicable.

5-5 COMMUNICATING WITH STUDENTS, FAMILIES AND OTHER AUDIENCES ABOUT STUDENT PROGRESS

The teacher:
- provides regular, specific and non-critical feedback to students.
- praises student successes when appropriate and provides corrective feedback and support when students do not respond correctly.
- limits the use of negative feedback and is careful to avoid personal criticism.
- provides frequent and graphic performance feedback to students.
- provides for parent involvement in student learning and assessment.

Students:
- are aware of their academic progress.
- have frequent opportunities to demonstrate their learning.

FOCUSED OBSERVATION INSTRUMENT #5

Assessing Student Learning

Name of Teacher: __Bob Instructor__

Subject/Grade Level: __8th/History__

Specific Content/Activity:
__Civil War/Reconstruction__

Date of Observation: __9/23/03__

Time of Observation: Begin: __8:30__

End: __8:55__ **(1)**

Number of Students in Class: __24__

Learning Objective: "Today, we're going to be talking about the South after the Civil War, Reconstruction."

Record the names (descriptions, seat assignment) of students who were assessed. Circle the **+** beside the name(s) of students whose participation was successful. Circle the **−** beside the name(s) of students whose participation was not successful. Record the teacher's response to the student's response/performance/demonstration.

STUDENT	QUESTION	SUCCESSFUL/ UNSUCCESSFUL	TEACHER RESPONSE TO STUDENT
1. Paul	"Why is this period called Reconstruction?"	+ (−) ?	"OK. Steve, do you know?" **(2)**
2. Steve	"OK. Steve, do you know?"	+ (−) ?	"No, not exactly. Mariana, do you know?"
3. Mariana	"Mariana, do you know?"	(+) − ?	"That's a good answer. Did everybody get that?"
4. Audrey	"Why did they disenfranchise the Southerners?"	+ (−) ?	"Didn't you read the assignment?" (calls on Aaron)
5. Aaron	(same question to Aaron)	+ (−) ?	(student asks for definition of disenfranchisement) "Look it up." (calls on Mariana)
6. Mariana	(same question to Mariana)	(+) − ?	"Right again, Mariana. You guys better be paying attention because this stuff is going to be on the test." (calls on Aaron: "I'm going to give you another chance.")
7. Aaron	"What was the difference between Federal fiscal policy and fiscal policy in other Southern states?"	+ (−) ?	"Not hardly, Aaron. Does anybody know?" (Aaron puts handout in folder and puts down pen. Mr. I. calls on Mariana)
8. Mariana	(same question to Mariana)	(+) − ?	"I'm glad one person read the assignment, Mariana." (Mr. I. continues to lecture)
9. Matt	"Why were former Southern troops assigned the job of fighting Indians on the frontier?"	+ (−) ?	(following Mr. I.'s question, Matt asks, "I'm sorry, what?") "You sure are." Mr. I. then calls on Paul)
10. Paul	(same question to Paul)	(+) − ?	"Right, Paul. See what happens when you pay attention?"

Note: Teacher stood behind lectern for entire period.

Instructional Strategies Used to Assess Student Learning

Check any techniques that the teacher uses to assess student learning. Checking the technique does not necessarily mean that the technique was used effectively—it simply means that the technique was used. Write notes or comments that will help you to remember what the teacher did/ failed to do.

(3)

_X_ The teacher verbally monitors/assesses individual students (random questioning, interacting during group/seatwork).

____ The teacher physically monitors individual students (walking around the class, examining students' work).

____ The teacher monitors group work, ensuring that that all/almost all students are participating and mastering the content.

____ The teacher implements formal/informal pre- and post instruction assessment strategies.

____ The teacher incorporates formative assessment strategies (paper/pencil, performances, demonstrations).

____ The teacher adjusts instruction in response to assessment results.

____ The teacher reteaches as needed when assessment strategies indicate that some or all students have not mastered the content.

_X_ The teacher provides positive feedback to successful responses/performances (verbal and/or nonverbal).   _Reinforced Mariana's responses_

____ The teacher provides specific corrective feedback to unsuccessful students.

____ The teacher provides process feedback that demonstrates how to achieve the correct response.

____ The teacher prompts/assists students who are having difficulty responding/performing.

____ Other technique(s)

Summary of Data and Evaluation on Assessing Student Learning

In the space below, summarize the data from the previous two pages and make evaluations about the quality of instructional strategies.

Student Success   **(4)**

1. How many students participated? __6__ of __24__ participated.

2. How many students were successful? __2__ of __6__ who participated.

3. How many students were unsuccessful? __4__ of __6__ who participated.

What was the learning objective?
"Today, we're going to be talking about the South after the Civil War, Reconstruction."

What assessment strategies were used?
Random questioning for six students.

Were the assessment strategies aligned with the lesson's objectives and instruction?
Questions about the South after the Civil War.

Based on the data, which statements best describe what you observed?   **(5)**

The number(s) in parentheses indicate the component(s) of the fifth standard that is or is not being met.

Meets Standards	Does Not Meet Standards	Notes
____ Learning objectives are clearly communicated (5-1).	_X_ Learning objectives are unclear (5-1).	*No statement of objective; statement of activity*
____ The teacher moves through the room when monitoring seatwork and/or independent practice (5-2).	_X_ The teacher is stationary and does not monitor students' seatwork and/or independent practice (5-2).	*Mr. I. remained behind lectern for most of instruction*
____ The teacher monitors students' responses in order to assess their understanding and success (5-2).	_X_ The teacher does not monitor students' responses in order to assess their understanding and success (5-2).	*Mr. I. ignores incorrect responses and student questions*
____ The teacher provides process feedback that shows students how to achieve the correct answer (5-4; 5-5).	_X_ The teacher does not provide process feedback that shows students how to achieve the correct answer (5-4; 5-5).	*When students respond incorrectly, Mr. I. calls on another student*
_X_ The teacher provides positive feedback to correct responses (5-3; 5-5).	____ The teacher does not provide positive feedback to correct responses (5-3; 5-5).	*To Marianna "That's a good answer"*
_X_ Most students who receive positive feedback repeat their participation and success (5-3).	____ Most students who receive positive feedback do not repeat their participation and success (5-3).	*Marianna participates repeatedly*

____ The teacher provides supportive, non-critical feedback to incorrect responses (5-3; 5-5).	X The teacher provides negative, non-supportive feedback to incorrect responses (5-3; 5-5).	To incorrect responses Mr. I. says: "Why not?" Didn't you read the assignment?" "Look it up," "Not hardly, Does anybody know?" "You sure are" (To a student who says "I'm sorry.")
____ Most students who receive corrective feedback continue to participate and are successful (5-3).	____ Most students who receive corrective feedback do not continue to participate and are successful (5-3).	
____ Assessment strategies are aligned with course objectives and instruction (5-2; 5-4).	____ Assessment strategies are not aligned with course objectives and instruction (5-2; 5-4).	
____ Assessment strategies allow students to demonstrate their understanding of content in meaningful ways (5-2; 5-3).	X Assessment strategies do not allow students to demonstrate their understanding of content in meaningful ways (5-2; 5-3).	Students answer questions; no other assessment strategies used.
____ The teacher incorporates pre- and post- instruction assessment strategies (5-2; 5-4).	____ The teacher does not incorporate pre- and post- instruction assessment strategies (5-2; 5-4).	
____ The teacher reteaches when students fail to master the content (5-2; 5-3).	X The teacher does not reteach when students fail to master the content (5-2; 5-3).	No reviewing or reteaching of key concepts when students demonstrated difficulty
____ The teacher implements corrective strategies following instruction and/or testing (5-4).	X The teacher does not implement corrective strategies following instruction and/or testing (5-4).	

Commentary

(1) In the first section of the instrument, Ima records some of the basic information that she will need when she is ready to write her memorandum to Mr. Instructor (e.g., the date, time, and length of the observation, etc.).

(2) In this section, she records each teacher/student interaction as it occurs. Ima is interested in the number of students who are assessed and the type of feedback Bob gives them. Paul's response was incorrect and Mr. Instructor called on Steve. When Steve answered incorrectly, Mr. Instructor called on Mariana. Mariana's response was correct and Mr. Instructor told her that she had a "good answer." When Audrey did not know an answer, Mr. Instructor asked, "Why not? Didn't you read the assignment?"

Note: All information is presented in objective, non-judgmental terms. Ima doesn't include judgmental or editorial comments. When Mr. Instructor responds to Audrey, "Why not? Didn't you read the assignment?" Ima recorded his exact words rather than the inappropriate judgment "put-down comment by teacher." In recording observation data and writing documentation, Ima wisely sticks to the facts.

(3) This section of the instrument is completed in the classroom during "down time"; that is, when there are few teacher/student interactions and when Ima has time to consider other things happening in the classroom. She checks the assessment strategies that Bob uses and takes notes that will later tell her whether or not they were effective.

(4) The final part of the focused observation instrument should be completed outside of the classroom. It consists of a summary of the data and evaluations from the previous two sections of the instrument. Remember that the preceding data were factual and objective — no judgments were made about the quality or effectiveness of the teaching behaviors. In completing this section, Ima summarizes the data and evaluates Bob's performance. In the case of Mr. Instructor, the summary reveals the following:

- Six of the twenty-four students were verbally monitored/assessed through teacher questions.

- Two of the six who were assessed were successful. Three of the four correct responses came from Mariana.

- Eighteen of the twenty-four students were not verbally monitored or assessed.

- Mr. Instructor did not communicate the learning objective. His statement, "Today we're going to be talking about the South after the Civil War, Reconstruction" was a statement of the activity, not a statement of the learning objective against which he and the students could assess progress.

- The only assessment strategy that was used was "verbally monitors/assesses individual students (random questioning . . .)." Ima's note, "6 monitored/assessed" provides the data that will later serve as the basis for her evaluation.

(5) The sections labeled "Meets Standards" and "Does Not Meet Standards" provide a contrast of evaluations based on the data from the observation. Ima may find this language useful when she is completing her focused observation memorandum.

Writing a Focused Observation Memorandum

Ima is now ready to write a memorandum to communicate the content of her evaluation to Bob. Ima has not included professional growth activities in this memorandum. If Bob has not improved when she revisits his classroom in two weeks, she may direct Bob to complete growth activities or develop a formal professional growth plan.

Surfs Up Unified School District
1234 Sunny Lane
Surfs Up, CA 90000

TO: Mr. Bob Instructor

FROM: Dr. Ima Leader

DATE: September 29, 2003

SUBJECT: Report of Classroom Observation

This memorandum will formally communicate information gathered during my observation of September 23, 2003. I observed from 8:30 to 8:55 while you conducted a lesson on post-Civil War Reconstruction with a group of 24 eighth graders.

You began by telling the students that it would be important to take notes because much of the information was not available from the assigned reading. During the remainder of my visit, I observed the following:

1. Six of the 24 students were verbally monitored/ assessed through teacher questions.

2. Two of the six who were assessed were successful. Three of the four correct responses came from Mariana.

3. Eighteen of the 24 students were <u>not</u> verbally monitored or assessed.

4. Students who were not successful did not receive prompting or corrective feedback. When students were unsuccessful, you immediately called on a different student or said:

   - "Why not? Didn't you read the assignment?"

   - "Look it up" (in response to a student who asked what a word meant).

- "Not hardly. Does anybody know?"
- " You sure are" (in response to a student who asked "I'm sorry, what?").

5. You remained at the lectern during the entire lesson.

6. You did not provide any re-teaching of any part of the lesson.

The Surfs Up U.S.D. appraisal system has the expectation that you monitor and assess student learning. Within that evaluation standard, there is an expectation that you (1) establish and communicate learning goals to students; (2) monitor and assess the progress of all students; (3) provide prompting and corrective feedback to students who are unsuccessful in ways that support their success; and (4) adjust instruction or re-teach when formative assessment indicates that students are not successful.

The data from my observation indicate that these expectations related to assessment of student learning were not met. If you have questions or concerns regarding these expectations, please contact the PAR consulting teacher for the social studies department, Ms. Lenda Hand.

I will be observing in your classroom again beginning two weeks from today. In all future observations I will expect you to utilize appropriate assessment strategies and to provide appropriate feedback and support to students who respond incorrectly.

Copy: PAR Council

Ms. Lenda Hand

My signature verifies that I have received a copy of this memorandum. It does not necessarily mean that I agree with the content. I understand that I have the right to present a written response within ten working days.

_____   _____

/s/ Bob Instructor   Date

SUMMARY AND CONCLUSION

In this chapter we have presented a focused observation instrument related to the fifth CSTP standard, Assessing Student Learning, and demonstrated its use during Bob Instructor's lesson on Reconstruction.

Throughout this handbook we have emphasized that gathering classroom documentation information during 15-30 minute walk-throughs observations need not be a difficult task. The focused observation instruments we have presented simplify the documentation process by allowing administrators and consulting teachers to concentrate on particular aspects of instruction in which a teacher may be experiencing difficulty. By focusing the evaluator's attention on one area of instruction, the instruments facilitate effective documentation.

Principals and others in supervisory roles will find that the information gathered with a focused observation instrument is easily incorporated in follow-up memoranda and professional growth plans. Adding remediation activities and assessment language linked to expected changes in student behavior in these documents helps assure teaching improvement and enables schools to meet the No Child Left Behind Act's requirement of having a highly qualified teacher in every classroom. If improvement is not forthcoming, the groundwork is laid for possible reassignment or even contract termination.

While peer coaches and consulting teachers probably will not write memoranda and professional growth plans, we believe that they will find the focused observation instruments useful in gathering observation data and conducting conferences with teachers. The information collected with the focused observation instruments also will be useful when consulting teachers report to PAR committees and/or provide evidence of support and improvement to supervisors.

APPENDIX A

Appendix A includes blank versions of the five focused observation instruments discussed in this handbook. The copyright for the hand book has been waived to the extent that purchasers may want to make copies of the forms for their use. The authors assume no responsibility for any liability that may arise from their use.

FOCUSED OBSERVATION INSTRUMENT #1

Engaging and Supporting All Students In Learning

Name of Teacher: _____   **Date of Observation:** _____

Subject/Grade Level: _____   **Time of Observation: Begin:** _____

Specific Content/Activity: **End:** _____

                                                                       Number of Students in Class: _____

Learning Objective:

Record the names (descriptions, seat assignment) of students who were assessed. Circle the **+** beside the name(s) of students whose participation was succussful. Circle the **–** beside the name(s) of students whose participation was not successful. Record the teacher's response to the student's response/performance/demonstration.

STUDENT	QUESTION	SUCCESSFUL/ UNSUCCESSFUL	TEACHER RESPONSE TO STUDENT
1.		+ – ?	
2.		+ – ?	
3.		+ – ?	
4.		+ – ?	
5.		+ – ?	
6.		+ – ?	
7.		+ – ?	
8.		+ – ?	
9.		+ – ?	
10.		+ – ?	

Instructional Strategies Used to Promote and Support Student Engagement

Check any techniques that the teacher uses to promote active, successful student engagement in learning. Checking the technique does not necessarily mean that the technique was used effectively—it simply means that the technique was used. Write notes or comments that will help you to remember what the teacher did/failed to do.

_____ The teacher facilitates connections between new knowledge and prior knowledge, other subject areas and/or students' own experiences.

_____ The teacher reviews the content of previous lessons in establishing the context for current instruction.

_____ The teacher provides opportunities for students to volunteer, offer feedback and make independent choices.

_____ The teacher provides frequent opportunities for students to actively participate in the lesson.

_____ The teacher structures questions to maximize student success.

_____ The teacher varies the cognitive level of questions to accommodate students of different ability levels.

_____ The teacher positively reinforces student participation and success.

_____ The teacher encourages slow/reluctant learners.

_____ Instructional activities and materials are varied.

_____ Instructional activities and materials relate to students' interests and needs.

_____ Instructional activities allow/encourage students to interact with each other.

_____ Instructional activities include opportunities for independent student practice.

_____ Instructional activities emphasize problem solving, critical thinking, analysis, and/or other higher order thinking skills.

_____ Other technique(s)

Summary of Data and Evaluation of Student Engagement and Learning

In the space below, summarize the data from the previous two pages and evaluate the level of instructional support for student engagement and learning.

Active Student Participation and Success

1. How many students participated? _____ of _____ participated.

2. How many students were successful? _____ of _____ who participated.

3. How many students were unsuccessful? _____ of _____ who participated.

What was the learning objective?

What instructional activities, strategies, and resources were implemented in teaching the lesson?

Based on the data, which statements best describe what you observed?

The number(s) in parentheses indicate the component of the first standard that is or is not being met.

Meets Standards

_____ All/almost all students were engaged and successful (all components).

_____ All/almost all students successfully made connections to prior knowledge, to other subject areas and to interests and experiences outside the classroom (1-1).

_____ All/almost all students successfully participated in problem solving, critical thinking and application activities (1-4).

_____ All/almost all students engaged in self-directed/self-motivated learning (1-5).

_____ All/almost all students experienced opportunities for autonomous interaction and choice (1-3).

_____ Instruction incorporated a variety of strategies, activities and materials related to students' interests and needs (1-2).

_____ Instructional activities accommodated students of varying cognitive abilities (1-2).

Does Not Meet Standards

_____ Few/no students were engaged and successful (all components).

_____ Few/no students successfully made connections to prior knowledge, to other subject areas and to interests and experiences outside the classroom (1-1).

_____ Few/no students successfully participated in problem solving, critical thinking and application activities (1-4).

_____ Few/no students engaged in self-directed/self-motivated learning (1-5).

_____ Few/no students experienced opportunities for autonomous interaction and choice (1-3).

_____ Instruction did not incorporate a variety of strategies, activities and materials related to students' interests and needs (1-2).

_____ Instructional activities did not accommodate students of varying cognitive abilities (1-2).

Learner Centered Instruction

Name of Teacher: _____

Date of Observation: _____

Subject/Grade Level: _____

Time of Observation: Begin: _____

Specific Content/Activity: _____

End: _____

Number of Students in Class: _____

Learning Objective:

Document the active participation of students. Enter ✓+ if the student was successful and ✓- if the student was unsuccessful. Use arrows to record student-student exchanges as well as teacher-student dialogue. Make notes to jog your memory about the content of discussion and teacher responses to students' questions, performances, and behavior.

FOCUSED OBSERVATION INSTRUMENT #2

Creating and Maintaining Effective Environments for Student Learning

Name of Teacher: _____

Subject/Grade Level: _____

Specific Content/Activity:

Date of Observation: _____

Time of Observation: Begin: _____

End: _____

Number of Students in Class: _____

The statements on the left reflect effective learning environments that meet standards, and those on the right reflect learning environments that do not meet standards. Check the statements that best describe your observations. Include notes that detail and/or support your observations.

Creating a Physical Environment that Engages All Students

Meets Standards	Does Not Meet Standards	Notes
____ The classroom environment is orderly and safe.	____ The classroom environment is disorderly and/or unsafe.	
____ The classroom arrangement permits student movement with a minimum of disruption.	____ The classroom arrangement inhibits student movement and increases the likelihood of disruption.	
____ The classroom arrangement permits the teacher maximum visibility of students.	____ The classroom arrangement limits the teacher's visibility of students.	
____ The seating plan maximizes visibility of instructional areas and facilitates student participation.	____ The seating plan limits student visibility of instructional areas and discourages student participation.	

Establishing a Climate that Promotes Fairness and Respect

Meets Standards	Does Not Meet Standards	Notes
____ The teacher uses student names.	____ The teacher does not use student names.	
____ The teacher uses a positive and/or patient vocal tone.	____ The teacher uses a negative and/or impatient vocal tone.	
____ The teacher applies rules rules consistently and fairly.	____ The teacher applies rules inconsistently and unfairly.	
____ The teacher encourages student participation and respects student contributions.	____ The teacher does not encourage student participation and/or ignores student contributions.	
____ The teacher interacts positively with students and is supportive.	____ The teacher ignores or is impatient with students experiencing difficulty.	
____ The teacher provides corrective feedback that preserves student dignity.	____ The teacher provides negative/demeaning corrective feedback.	

Promoting Social Development and Group Responsibility

Meets Standards	Does Not Meet Standards	Notes
____ The teacher conveys an expectation of student attention, cooperation and responsibility.	____ The teacher does not convey an expectation of student attention, cooperation and responsibility.	
____ Classroom procedures emphasize productive use of time and support student accountability.	____ Classroom procedures do not emphasize productive use of time and do not support student accountability.	

Establishing and Maintaining Standards for Student Behavior

Meets Standards	Does Not Meet Standards	Notes
____ Classroom rules and procedures are clearly posted and consistently enforced.	____ Classroom rules and procedures are not clearly posted and inconsistently enforced.	
____ The teacher monitors student behavior and intervenes when inappropriate or disruptive behavior occurs.	____ The teacher does not monitor student behavior and fails to intervene when inappropriate or disruptive behavior occurs.	
____ The teacher provides specific feedback regarding appropriate/inappropriate student behavior.	____ The teacher does not provide specific feedback regarding appropriate/inappropriate student behavior.	
____ The teacher uses a variety of verbal and nonverbal signals to stop inappropriate behavior.	____ The teacher uses limited/ no verbal and nonverbal signals to stop inappropriate behavior.	

Planning and Implementing Classroom Procedures and Routines that Support Student Learning

Meets Standards	Does Not Meet Standards	Notes
____ Activities are structured to maintain appropriate pacing and student engagement.	____ Activities are not structured to maintain appropriate pacing and student engagement.	
____ The teacher provides clear instructions for class activities and during transitions between activities.	____ The teacher does not provide clear instructions for class activities and during transitions between activities.	
____ The teacher identifies and assists those students who do not understand instructions.	____ The teacher does not identify and assist those students who do not understand instructions.	
____ The teacher communicates the value of the lesson's content and activities.	____ The teacher fails to communicate the value of the lesson's content and activities.	

Using Instructional Time Effectively

Meets Standards	Does Not Meet Standards	Notes
____ Class begins promptly.	____ Class does not begin promptly.	
____ Classroom procedures facilitate maximum use of instructional time.	____ Classroom procedures do not facilitate maximum use of instructional time.	
____ The teacher makes full use of instructional time and minimizes interruptions.	____ The teacher does not make full use of instructional time and permits frequent interruptions.	

FOCUSED OBSERVATION INSTRUMENT #3

Understanding and Organizing Subject Matter for Student Learning

Name of Teacher: _____   Date of Observation: _____

Subject/Grade Level: _____   Time of Observation: Begin: _____

Specific Content/Activity: _____   End: _____

Number of Students in Class: _____

Describe the lesson's objective(s).

Mark each statement that best describes the lesson's activities.

___   new material with explanation/demonstration/modeling

___   practice/application/processing of material already taught

___   other (describe)

Circle the word(s) that reflects what you observe.

The lesson includes:

(accurate/inaccurate) subject matter content.

(logical/illogical) organization and (smooth/awkward) transitions between activities.

(opportunities/no opportunities) for higher level critical thinking and application activities.

sequencing that (supports/does not support) student understanding of the subject matter.

materials and resources that are (relevant/irrelevant) to the content and (appropriate/inappropriate) to students' development.

(correct/incorrect) written and spoken language.

Briefly describe the organization of the lesson.

Briefly describe the lesson's activities and their sequence.

What strategies does the teacher utilize to move students from the knowledge/comprehension to application of the skill or concept taught?

___ higher level questioning

___ group work

___ paper/pencil activity

___ performance/demonstration

___ independent products

___ other (describe)

Describe evidence that students are successful/unsuccessful in reaching the lesson's objectives.

Do students make connections between the current instruction and

___ prior learning?

___ other subject areas?

___ students' lives and experiences?

___ issues beyond the classroom?

How does the teacher provide for students to make connections?

___ The teacher tells/explains the connection.

___ The teacher facilitates a process (discussion, activity, etc.) through which students recognize connections.

List/describe the materials, resources and technologies incorporated into the lesson?

Summary of Data and Evaluation of Understanding and
Organizing Subject Matter for Student Learning

The statements on the left reflect classroom instruction that has effectively organized subject matter and content for student understanding and learning. These statements reflect classrooms that meet the requirements of third CSTP standard. The statements on the right reflect classroom instruction that do not meet standards. Include notes that detail and/or support your observations. The number(s) in parentheses indicate the component(s) of the third standard that is or is not being met.

Meets Standards	Does Not Meet Standards	Notes
____ The focus of instruction is clear (3-1; 3-2).	____ The focus of instruction is unclear (3-1; 3-2).	
____ Instructional content and/or skills are relevant and new (3-1).	____ Instructional content and/or skills are repetitive and/or irrelevant (3-1).	
____ The presentation of the subject matter is logical and clear (3-2).	____ The presentation of the subject matter is not logical or unclear (3-2).	
____ Learning is organized around the central themes/ concepts of the discipline (3-1; 3-3).	____ Learning is not organized around the central themes/ concepts of the discipline; learning is miscellaneous and unconnected (3-1; 3-3).	
____ The critical attributes of the concept or skill being taught are elaborated in ways that lead to student mastery (3-1; 3-2; 3-3).	____ The critical attributes of the concept or skill being taught are unclear and students are unsuccessful (3-1; 3-2; 3-3).	
____ The teacher incorporates relevant examples, explanations and/or demonstrations of the subject matter (3-3; 3-4; 3-5).	____ The teacher does not incorporate relevant examples, explanations and/or demonstrations of the subject matter (3-3; 3-4; 3-5).	
____ The teacher repeats information and responds appropriately to student questions (3-2).	____ The teacher does not repeat information and does not respond appropriately to student questions (3-2).	
____ The teacher teaches, reteaches and reviews as necessary (3-2).	____ The teacher does not teach, reteach and review as necessary (3-2).	
____ Students have opportunities to engage in critical thinking, problem solving and/or creative inquiry (3-3; 3-4).	____ Students do not have opportunities to engage in critical thinking, problem solving and/or creative inquiry (3-3; 3-4).	

Meets Standards	Does Not Meet Standards	Notes
____ Students have opportunities to connect/ apply learning to other disciplines, their own lives, and issues beyond the classroom (3-3; 3-4).	____ Students do not have opportunities to connect/ apply learning to other disciplines, their own lives, and issues beyond the classroom (3-3; 3-4).	
____ Students' active engagement and participation indicate that the lesson's content and activities are interesting (3-2; 3-5).	____ Students' lack of active engagement and participation indicate the the lesson's content and activities are not interesting (3-2; 3-5).	
____ Content and instructional strategies represent the current/best practice within the subject area (3-1; 3-4).	____ Content and instructional strategies do not represent the current/best practice within the subject area (3-1; 3-4).	
____ Instructional materials relate to the subject matter and are relevant to students' interests and needs (3-2; 3-5).	____ Instructional materials do not relate to the subject matter and/or are not relevant to students' interests and needs (3-2; 3-5).	
____ Relevant technology is incorporated, when appropriate, in the lesson (3-5).	____ Relevant and appropriate use of technology is omitted from the lesson (3-5).	
____ The course objectives, instruction and assessment are aligned (3-1; 3-4).	____ The course objectives, instruction and assessment are not aligned (3-1; 3-4).	

FOCUSED OBSERVATION INSTRUMENT #4

Planning Instruction and Designing Learning Experiences for All Students

Name of Teacher: _____   **Date(s) of Review:** _____

Subject/Grade Level: _____   **Number of Students:** _____

Course Content or Unit of Study:

Review the lesson plans for dates cited above and check the statements that best describe your observations. The number(s) in parentheses indicate the component(s) of the fourth standard that is or is not being met.

Meets Standards	Does Not Meet Standards	Notes
____ Lesson plans are completed in accordance with district policies and campus level requirments.	____ Lesson plans are not completed in accordance with district policies and campus level requirments.	
____ Learning objectives are clearly stated (4-2).	____ Learning objectives are unclear (4-2).	
____ Lesson plans outline the presentation of relevant and new content and/or skills (4-3).	____ Lesson plans do not outline the presentation of relevant and new content and/or skills (4-3).	
____ Lesson content is organized around the central themes/concepts of the discipline (4-3).	____ Lesson content is not organized around the central themes/concepts of the discipline (4-3).	
____ Lesson plans include activities that allow students to engage in critical thinking, problem solving and/or creative inquiry (4-3).	____ Lesson plans do not include activities that allow students to engage in critical thinking, problem solving and/or creative inquiry (4-3).	
____ The lesson(s)' activities are appropriate for students' developmental level and abilities (4-1).	____ The lesson(s)' activities are inappropriate for students' developmental level and abilities (4-1).	
____ Lesson plans include activities and materials that are related to students' interests and needs (4-1).	____ Lesson plans do not include activities and materials that are related to students' interests and needs (4-1).	
____ Lesson plans include activities that allow students to connect/apply learning to other disciplines, their own lives and issues beyond the classroom (4-1).	____ Lesson plans do not include activities that allow students to connect/apply learning to other disciplines, their own lives and issues beyond the classroom (4-1).	
____ The lesson's activities are differentiated for students of varying abilities. (4-5).	____ The lesson's activities are not differentiated for students of varying abilities. (4-5).	
____ The lesson plans show evidence of short and long term planning (4-4).	____ The lesson plans do not show evidence of short and long term planning (4-4).	
____ The lesson plans reflect accommodations for students' individual needs (4-5).	____ The lesson plans do not reflect accommodations for students' individual needs (4-5).	

FOCUSED OBSERVATION INSTRUMENT #5

Assessing Student Learning

Name of Teacher: _____   Date of Observation: _____

Subject/Grade Level: _____   Time of Observation: Begin: _____

Specific Content/Activity: _____   End: _____

Number of Students in Class: _____

Learning Objective:

Record the names (descriptions, seat assignment) of students who were assessed. Circle the **+** beside the name(s) of students whose participation was succussful. Circle the **–** beside the name(s) of students whose participation was not successful. Record the teacher's response to the student's response/performance/demonstration.

STUDENT	SUCCESSFUL/ QUESTION	UNSUCCESSFUL	TEACHER RESPONSE TO STUDENT
1.		+ – ?	
2.		+ – ?	
3.		+ – ?	
4.		+ – ?	
5.		+ – ?	
6.		+ – ?	
7.		+ – ?	
8.		+ – ?	
9.		+ – ?	
10.		+ – ?	

Instructional Strategies Used to Assess Student Learning

Check any techniques that the teacher uses to assess student learning. Checking the technique does not necessarily mean that the technique was used effectively—it simply means that the technique was used. Write notes or comments that will help you to remember what the teacher did/failed to do.

_____ The teacher verbally monitors/assesses individual students (random questioning, interacting during group/seatwork).

_____ The teacher physically monitors individual students (walking around the class, examining students' work).

_____ The teacher monitors group work, ensuring that that all/almost all students are participating and mastering the content.

_____ The teacher implements formal/informal pre- and post instruction assessment strategies.

_____ The teacher incorporates formative assessment strategies (paper/pencil, performances, demonstrations).

_____ The teacher adjusts instruction in response to assessment results.

_____ The teacher reteaches as needed when assessment strategies indicate that some or all students have not mastered the content.

_____ The teacher provides positive feedback to successful responses/performances (verbal and/or nonverbal).

_____ The teacher provides specific corrective feedback to unsuccessful students.

_____ The teacher provides process feedback that demonstrates how to achieve the correct response.

_____ The teacher prompts/assists students who are having difficulty responding/performing.

_____ Other technique(s)

Summary of Data and Evaluation on Assessing Student Learning

In the space below, summarize the data from the previous two pages and make evaluations about the quality of instructional strategies.

Student Success

1. How many students participated? _____ of _____ participated.

2. How many students were successful? _____ of _____ who participated.

3. How many students were unsuccessful? _____ of _____ who participated.

What was the learning objective?

What assessment strategies were used?

Were the assessment strategies aligned with the lesson's objectives and instruction?

Based on the data, which statements best describe what you observed?

The number(s) in parentheses indicate the component(s) of the fifth standard that is or is not being met.

Meets Standards	Does Not Meet Standards	Notes
____ Learning objectives are clearly communicated (5-1).	____ Learning objectives are unclear (5-1).	
____ The teacher moves through the room when monitoring seatwork and/or independent practice (5-2).	____ The teacher is stationary and does not monitor students' seatwork and/or independent practice (5-2).	
____ The teacher monitors students' responses in order to assess their understanding and success (5-2).	____ The teacher does not monitor students' responses in order to assess their understanding and success (5-2).	
____ The teacher provides process feedback that shows students how to achieve the correct answer (5-4; 5-5).	____ The teacher does not provide process feedback that shows students how to achieve the correct answer (5-4; 5-5).	
____ The teacher provides positive feedback to correct responses (5-3; 5-5).	____ The teacher does not provide positive feedback to correct responses (5-3; 5-5).	

Meets Standards	Does Not Meet Standards	Notes
____ Most students who receive positive feedback repeat their participation and success (5-3).	____ Most students who receive positive feedback do not repeat their participation and success (5-3).	
____ The teacher provides supportive, non-critical feedback to incorrect responses (5-3; 5-5).	____ The teacher provides negative, non-supportive feedback to incorrect responses (5-3; 5-5).	
____ Most students who receive corrective feedback continue to participate and are successful (5-3).	____ Most students who receive corrective feedback do not continue to participate and are successful (5-3).	
____ Assessment strategies are aligned with course objectives and instruction (5-2; 5-4).	____ Assessment strategies are not aligned with course objectives and instruction (5-2; 5-4).	
____ Assessment strategies allow students to demonstrate their understanding of content in meaningful ways (5-2; 5-3).	____ Assessment strategies do not allow students to demonstrate their understanding of content in meaningful ways (5-2; 5-3).	
____ The teacher incorporates pre- and post- instruction assessment strategies (5-2; 5-4).	____ The teacher does not incorporate pre- and post- instruction assessment strategies (5-2; 5-4).	
____ The teacher reteaches when students fail to master the content (5-2; 5-3).	____ The teacher does not reteach when students fail to master the content (5-2; 5-3).	
____ The teacher implements corrective strategies following instruction and/or testing (5-4).	____ The teacher does not implement corrective strategies following instruction and/or testing (5-4).	

APPENDIX B:
RULES OF CONDUCT OF PROFESSIONAL EDUCATORS
TITLE 5, CALIFORNIA CODE OF REGULATIONS §§ 80331 ET SEQ.

§ 80331.   General

(a) These rules are binding upon every person holding a credential or any license to perform educational services under the jurisdiction of the Commission on Teacher Credentialing, and the consequences of any willful breach my be revocation or suspension of the credential, or license, or private admonition of the holder.

(b) Nothing in these rules is intended to limit or supersede any provision of law relating to the duties and obligations of certificated persons or to the consequences of the violation of such duties and obligations. The prohibition of certain conduct in these rules is not to be interpreted as approval of conduct not specifically cited.

(c) These rules may be cited and referred to as "Rules of Conduct for Professional Educators."

(d) [Dated]

(e) As used in these rules:

(1) "Certificated person" means any person who hold a certificate, permit, credential, or other license authorizing the performance of teaching or education related service in grades K through 12 in California public schools.

(2) "Professional employment" means the performance for compensation of teaching or other eduction-related employment in a position for which certification requirements are set by law.

(3) "Confidential information" means information which was provided to the certificated person solely for the purpose of facilitating his/her performance of professional services for or on behalf of the person or employer providing such information.

§ 80332.   Professional Candor and Honesty in Letters or Memoranda of Employment Recommendation.

(a) A certificated person shall not write or sign any letter or memorandum which intentionally omits significant facts, or which states as facts matters which the writer does not know of his/her own knowledge to be true relating to the professional qualifications or personal fitness to perform certificated services of any person whom the writer knows will use the letter or memorandum to obtain professional employment nor shall he/she agree to provide a positive letter of recommendation which misrepresents facts as a condition of resignation or for withdrawing action against the employing agency.

(b) This rule has no application to statements identified in the letter or memorandum as personal opinions of the writer but does apply to unqualified statements as fact that which the writer does not know to be true or to statements as fact that which the writer knows to be true or to statements as fact that which the writes knows to be untrue.

§ 80333. Withdrawal from Professional Employment.

(a) A certificated person shall not abandon professional employment without good cause.

(b) "Good Cause" includes but is not necessarily limited to circumstances not caused by or under the voluntary control of the certificated person.

§ 80334. Unauthorized Private Gain or Advantage.

A certificated person shall not:

(a) Use for his/her own private gain or advantage or to prejudice the rights or benefits of another person any confidential information relating to students or fellow professionals;

(b) Use for his/her own private gain or advantage the time, facilities equipment, or supplies which is the property of his/her employer without the express or clearly implied permission of his/her employer;

(c) Accept any compensation or benefit or thing of value other than his/her regular compensation for the performance of any service which he/she is required to render in the course and scope of his/her certificated employment. This rule shall not restrict performance of any overtime or supplemental services at the request of the school employer; nor shall it apply to or restrict the acceptance of gifts or tokens of minimal value offered and accepted openly from students, parents or other persons in recognition or appreciation of services.

§ 80335. Performance of Unauthorized Professional Services

A certificated person shall not, after July 1, 1989:

(a) Knowingly, accept an assignment to perform professional services if he or she does not possess a credential authorizing the service to be performed; unless he or she has first exhausted any existing local remedies to correct the situation, has then notified the county superintendent of schools in writing of the incorrect assignment, and the county superintendent of schools has made a determination, within 45 days of receipt of the notification, that the assignment was caused by extraordinary circumstances which make correction impossible, pursuant to the procedures referred to in Education Code Section 44258.9 (g)(2) and (3).

(b) Knowingly and willfully assign or require a subordinate certificated person to perform any professional service which the subordinate is not authorized to perform by his or her credential or which is not approved by appropriate governing board authorization, unless he or she has made reasonable attempts to correct the situation but has been unsuccessful, and has notified the county superintendent of schools of those attempts, and the county superintendent of schools has determined, within 45 days of being notified of the assignment, that the assignment was caused by extraordinary circumstances which make correction impossible.

(c) neither (a) nor (b) shall be applicable in a situation where extraordinary circumstances make the correction of the misassignment impossible.

(d) There shall be no adverse action taken against a certificated person under this rule for actions attributable to circumstances beyond his or her control.

(e) Effective October 20, 1993, no adverse action described in Title 5, California Code of Regulations, section 80331 (a) shall be imposed for violation of this provision prior to review and attempted disposition pursuant to Title 5, California Code of Regulations, sections 80339 through 80339.6.

§ 80336. Performance with Impaired Faculties.

(a) a certificated person shall not:

(1) Perform or attempt to perform any duties or services authorized by his or her credential during any period in which he or she knows or is in possession of facts showing that his or her mental or intellectual faculties are substantially impaired for any reason, including but not limited to use of alcohol or any controlled substance.

(2) Assign or require or permit a subordinate certificated person to perform any duties authorized by his or her credential during any period in which the superior certificated person knows of his or her own knowledge or is in possession of facts showing that the subordinate certificated person's mental or intellectual faculties are substantially impaired for any reason, including but not limited to use of alcohol or any controlled substance.

(b) For the purpose of this rule, substantial impairment means a visible inability to perform the usual and customary duties of the position in a manner that does not represent a danger to pupils, employees, or school property. It does no include or mean inability attributable to lack of, or inadequate, professional preparation or education.

§ 80337. Harassment and Retaliation Prohibited.

No certificated person shall directly or indirectly use or threaten to use any official authority or influence in any manner whatsoever which tends to discourage, restrain, interfere with, coerce, or discriminate against any subordinate or any certificated person who in good faith reports, discloses, divulges, or otherwise brings to the attention of the governing board of a school district, the Commission on Teacher Credentialing of any other public agency authorized to take remedial action, any facts or information relative to actual or suspected violation of any law regulating the duties of persons serving in the public school system, including but not limited to these rules of professional conduct.

§ 80338. Discrimination Prohibited.

A certificated person shall not, without good cause, in the course and scope of his or her certificated employment and solely because of race, color, creed, gender, national origin, handicapping condition or sexual orientation, refuse or fail to perform certificated services for any person.

§ 80339. [Remaining sections specify the procedure for addressing allegations of performance of unauthorized duties.]

APPENDIX C:
A GENERIC LIST OF REMEDIATION ACTIVITIES

THE TEACHER WILL . . .

- Develop a written strategy to . . .
- Develop a list of ways to . . .
- Provide a list of guided practice activities for . . .
- Prepare a list of directions for . . .
- List appropriate sponge activities to accompany . . .
- Develop and teach a lesson that . . .
- Review and summarize a list of possible techniques for . . .
- Tape record a class evidencing . . .
- Videotape a class evidencing . . .
- Watch and write a review of the teaching film, _____.
- Complete the following instrument, _____.
- Review selected instructional leadership materials in the area of remediation and write:
    - a summary statement of content.
    - a critique including how this information specifically can apply to teacher's classroom.
- Develop a task analysis . . .
- Define and give a rationale for the sequence of instruction.
- Outline a step-by-step plan for improving . . .
- Develop a schedule for . . .
- Prepare a list of . . . (e.g., positive feedback remarks).
- Develop a system of . . . (e.g., scheduled feedback, rewards).
- Create a sample list of questions that . . . (e.g., extend students' responses).
- Develop a questioning strategy based on Bloom's Taxonomy.
- Write instructional objectives, methods/procedures, student activities, and evaluation strategies.
- Write behavioral objectives in relation to . . .

- Review objectives and determine which are relevant to the ability level(s) of the students.
- Review available classroom materials and submit a chart determining which materials are relevant to the ability level(s) of the students.
- Prepare a list of materials to be used and state a rationale for each.
- Prepare a list of supplementary materials.
- Develop and implement a questionnaire for students concerning . . .
- Survey students' interests and abilities and group them for instruction.
- Identify the ability levels of your students.
- Develop a plan to determine the instructional needs of the students.
- Discuss the students' needs with the resource teacher.
- Establish rules, procedures, and consequences with students.
- Post in the room . . . (e.g., rules and consequences).
- Schedule to observe other teachers who . . .
- Attend a workshop on . . .
- Attend an on-campus meeting of teachers to brainstorm ways to improve . . .
- Invite the supervisor to visit . . .
- Develop a plan following these steps:
    - review and discuss curriculum goals
    - identify content focus and learning outcomes
    - identify student needs
    - select materials.
- Write a summary statement of how the lesson fits the focus and desired learner outcomes.
- Write objectives, methods, student activities, and evaluation strategy.
- Submit _____ to the evaluator.
- Write and submit lesson plans that include . . . (e.g., time allocations).
- Write and submit lesson plans designed to . . . (e.g., motivate students for learning).
- Write a self-critique or evaluation after the next three lessons, emphasizing . . .

APPENDIX D: SAMPLE FORMS

The following sample forms are included in this section:

Complaint Form This form requires persons who have a complaint about a school employee to provide detailed information in writing that will enable the administrator to conduct an effective investigation.

Template for Focused Observation Memorandum This form is designed to guide you through the development of a simple instructional memorandum and can be placed on a computer disk for this purpose. Thereafter, all you need to do is fill in the necessary information.

Professional Growth Plan Form

The copyright protection for this handbook has been modified to the extent that purchasers of the book may reproduce the forms in this section for their own use. We advise that you contact the school district personnel administrator and/or school attorney before doing so to make sure that the forms are consistent with local policy and practice and conform to union contract provisions. The authors do not assume any responsibility for liability associated with their use.

COMPLAINT FORM

Name of person filing this complaint: _____

Address: _____

Statement involves complaint against whom: _____

Please state your specific complaint or complaints. Please describe in detail the events surrounding the complaint against the above-named person. Please include dates, times, locations, persons present, substance of statements, and conversations, etc. Please be as factual as possible. If you must express an opinion, please make it clear that you are doing so. Attach additional pages if necessary. _____

_____

_____

_____

_____

_____

_____

_____

_____

Please refer us to any persons having personal knowledge of the facts stated in this complaint.

_____

_____

_____

Please state the individual harm alleged and identify the person or persons alleged to be harmed, if other than yourself.

_____

_____

Please state what specific relief or resolution you are requesting.

_____

_____

_____

_____

Please attach copies of any written documentation that may assist us in resolving this complaint.

Note: When you are finished, please reread your statement in its entirety. Make any necessary changes and initial those changes. Then initial each sheet in the bottom righthand corner. Sign and date below.

"I affirm that the above statement is the truth to the best of my knowledge."

_____   _____
Signature   Date   Signature   Date
Person making statement   Person receiving statement

TEMPLATE FOR
FOCUSED OBSERVATION MEMORANDUM

Your School District
Address
Your Town, California 90000

_____

(date of memorandum)

_____

(name of teacher/employee

_____

(campus/site assigned)

Dear _____ :

This memorandum is to formally communicate information gathered during my observation in
your classroom on _____ . I observed from _____ to _____ .
                          (Date)   *(Beginning Time)*   *(Ending Time)*

During that time you were _____
                                      (Brief Description of Content and Activity)

_____ to/with _____ students. During that
                                                                (# of students)

observation I observed the following:

- *Objective narrative*
- *Free of judgmental language*
- *What the teacher said and did and what the students said and did*

Standard ____ of the California Standards for the Teaching Profession has an expectation that you

Criterion ____ on the School District Appraisal System has an expectation that you *("exact wording of the criterion-level holistic expectation.")*

The grade-level curriculum content standards require that you

Our campus improvement plan has an expectation that you *(component / initiative in campus improvement plan).*

District (Campus) Policy *(cite policy number)* has an expectation that you *(summary or quotation from policy).*

The data from my observation indicate that these expectations were not met.

In future classroom observations I will expect to see expectations met in the following ways:

1. Teacher Behavior	Linking Language	Student Behavior
2. Teacher Behavior	Linking Language	Student Behavior
3. Teacher Behavior	Linking Language	Student Behavior

Finally, I have arranged (I recommend) the following as support for your efforts to meet these expectations. You will (you may wish to consider):

    1. Professional Development Activity

    2. Professional Development Activity

Sincerely,

   / S /

Principal

My signature verifies that I have received a copy of this memorandum. My signature does not necessarily indicate agreement with the content. I understand that I have a right to respond in writing within ten (10) working days.

_____   _____

Signature of Teacher   */ S /*   Date

PROFESSIONAL GROWTH PLAN

School Year 20 ____ - 20 ____

School District: _____ Campus: _____

Teacher: _____ Assignment/Grade: _____

1. List area(s) related to the California Standards for the Teaching Profession in which improvement are needed. Establish priorities if two or more areas are listed.

2. Specify growth activities and dates for completion.

3. Specify evidence that will be used to determine whether professional growth activities have been completed.

4. Specify evidence that will be used to determine whether growth has occurred or is occurring.

My appraiser(s) and I have developed this Professional Growth Plan.

Teacher Signature _____ **Date** _____

Supervisor Signature _____ **Date** _____

Other Appraiser Signature _____ **Date** _____
(if applicable)

APPENDIX E: RESEARCH ON EFFECTIVE TEACHING

Both the California Standards for the Teaching Profession and the focused observation instruments in this handbook are based on effective practices research. This appendix provides a summary of that research for those who may wish to investigate further into a particular aspect of the teaching process.

Anderson, S. A. (1994). Synthesis of research on mastery learning. (ERIC Reproduction Document No. ED 382 567).

Anderson, L.M., Evertson, C.M., and Emmer, E.L. (1979). Dimensions in classroom management derived from recent research. In S. Dasho (Chair), Perspectives on classroom management research. Symposium presented at the annual meeting of the American Educational Research Association, San Francisco, CA. (ERIC Document No. ED 175 860).

Anderson, L. M., Stevens, D. D., Prawat, R S., & Nickerson, J. (1988). Classroom task environments and students' task-related beliefs. The Elementary School Journal, 88, 281-295.

Armstrong, T. (1994). Multiple intelligences in the classroom. Alexandria, VA: Association for Supervision and Curriculum Development.

Aspy, D., & Roebuck F. (1977). Kids don't learn from people they don't like. Amherst: Human Resource Development Press.

Ausubel, D. (1963). The psychology of meaningful verbal learning. New York: Grune and Stratton.

Beane, J. A. & Brodhagen, B. L. (2001). Teaching in middle schools. In V. Richardson (Ed.), Handbook of research on teaching (4th ed., pp. 1157-1174). Washington, DC: American Educational Research Association.

Bembry, K. L., Jordan, H. R., Gomez, E., Anderson, M.C., & Mendro, R.L. (1998). Policy implications of long-term teacher effects on student achievement. Paper presented at the 1998 annual meeting of the American Educational Research Association, San Diego, CA.

Berliner, D.C. (1984). The half-full glass: A review of the research on teaching. In P. Hosford (Ed.), Using what we know about teaching. Alexandria, VA: Association for Supervision and Curriculum.

Berliner, D., & Tikunoff, W. (1976). The California Beginning Teacher Evaluation Study: Overview of the ethnographic study. Journal of Teacher Education, 27 (1), 24-30.

Blegen, M.B. (2000, February). A day in the life of a teacher. Basic Education, 7-12.

Block, J. H. (1973). Teachers, teaching, and mastery learning. The Journal of the National Education Association, 63 (7), 30-36.

Block, J. H. and Burns, R.B. (1976). Mastery learning. In L.S. Shulman (Ed.), Review of research in educa-tion, Vol. 4. Itasca, IL: Peacock.

Bloom, B. S. (1986). What we're learning about teaching and learning: A summary of recent research. Principal, 66 (2), 6-10.

Borich, G.D., Kash, M.M., and Kemp, F.D. (1979). What the teacher effective research has to say about teaching practices and student performance. Austin, TX: Southwest Educational Development Laboratory. (ERIC Document No. ED 189 077).

Brookover, W. B., Beady, C., Flood, P., Schweitzer, J., & Wisenbaker, J. (1979). School social systems and student achievement: Schools can make a difference. Brooklyn, NY: Praeger Publishers.

Brophy, J. E., & Evertson, C. M. (1974). Process-product correlations in the Texas Teacher Effectiveness Study: Final report. Expanded version of paper read at the Annual Meeting of The

American Educational Research Association, Chicago, IL. (ERIC Document Reproduction Service No. ED 091394).

Burbules, N. C., & Bruce, B. C. (2001). Theory and research on teaching as dialogue. In V. Richardson (Ed.), Handbook of research on teaching (4th ed., pp. 1102-1121). Washington, DC: American Educational Research Association.

Butzin, S. M. (1992). Integrating technology into the classroom: Lessons from the project CIMD experience. Phi Delta Kappan, 74 (4), 330-333.

Capie, W., Ellett, C., & Johnson, C. (1980). Relating pupil achievement gains to ratings of secondary student teacher performance. Paper presented at the Eastern Educational Research Association, Norfolk, VA. (ERIC Document No. ED 185 023).

Capie, W., Tobin, K.G., and Bowell, M. (1980). Using science achievement to validate ratings of student-teacher competencies. Paper presented at the National Association for Research in Science Teaching, Boston. (ERIC Document No. ED 186 261).

Casey, M. B. (1990). A planning and problem-solving preschool model: The methodology of being a good learner. Early Childhood Research Quarterly, 5, 53-67.

Cawelti, G. (Ed.) (1999). Handbook of research on improving student achievement (2nd ed.). Arlington, VA: Educational Research Service.

Cooley, W. W., & Leinhardt, G. (1980). The instructional dimensions study. Educational Evaluation and Policy Analysis, 2 (1), 7-25.

Denton, J., Furtado, L., Wu, Y., & Shields, S. (1992, April). Evaluating a content-focused model of teacher preparation via: Classroom observations student perceptions and student performance. Paper presented at the American Educational Research Association Annual Meeting, San Francisco, CA.

Doyle, W. (1986). Classroom organization and management. In Merlin C. Wittrock (Ed.), Handbook of research on teaching, (3rd ed., pp. 392-432). New York: Macmillan.

Dunkin, M.J. and Biddle, B.J. (1974). The study of teaching. New York: Holt, Rinehart and Winston.

Dwyer, D. (1994). Apple classrooms of tomorrow: What we've learned. Educational Leadership, 51 (7), 4-10.

Edmonds, R. R. (1982). Programs of school improvement: An overview. Educational Leadership, 40 (3), 4-11.

Ellett, C.D., Capie, W., and Johnson, C.E. (1981). Further studies of the criterion-related validity of the Teacher Performance Assessment Instruments. Athens, GA: Teacher Performance Assessment Project.

Emmer, E.T., Evertson, C.M., & Anderson, L.M. (1980). Effective classroom management at the beginning of the school year. The Elementary School Journal, 80, 219-231.

Englert, C.S. (1984). Effective direct instruction practices in special education settings. Remedial and special education (RASE), 5 (2), 38-47.

Evertson, C.M., Anderson, C., Anderson, L.M., & Brophy, J. (1980). Relationships between classroom behaviors and student outcomes in junior high mathematics and English classes. American Educa-tional Research Journal, 17, 43-60.

Evertson, C.M. & Emmer, E. (1982). Effective management at the beginning of the school year in junior high classes. Journal of Educational Psychology, 74 (4), 485-498.

Evertson, C. M., Emmer, E. T., & Brophy, J. E. (1980). Predictors of effective teaching in junior high mathematics classrooms. Journal for Research in Mathematics Education, 11, 167-178.

Evertson, C. M., Emmer, E. T., Sanford, J. P., & Clements, B. S. (1983). Improving classroom management: An experiment in elementary classrooms. The Elementary School Journal, 84, 173-188.

Feiman-Nemser, S. (2001). Helping novices learn to teach: Lessons from an experienced support teacher. Journal of Teacher Education, 52 (1), 17-30.

Fisher, C. W. (1978). <u>Teaching behaviors, academic learning time and student achievement: Final Report of Phase III-B, Beginning Teachers Evaluation Study</u>. Technical Report v-1. San Francisco, CA: Far West Lab for Educational Research and Development. (ERIC Document Reproduction Service No. ED 183 525).

Fuchs, L. S., Fuchs, D., Hamlett, C. L., Phillips, N. B., & Bentz, J. (1994). Classwide curriculum-based measurement: Helping general educators meet the challenge of student diversity. <u>Exceptional Children, 60</u> (6), 518-537.

Fuchs, L. S., Fuchs, D. & Tindall G. (1986). Effects of mastery learning procedures on student achievement. <u>Journal of Educational Research, 79</u> (5), 286-291.

Good, T. & Grouws, D.A. (1977). <u>Teacher's manual: Missouri mathematics effectiveness project.</u> Columbia, MO: University of Missouri, Center for Research in Social Behavior.

Good, T., & Grouws, D.A. (1979). The Missouri mathematics effectiveness project: An experimental study in fourth-grade classrooms. <u>Journal of Educational Psychology, 71</u> (3), 355-362.

Gottfried, A. E. (1985). Academic intrinsic motivation on elementary and junior high school students. <u>Journal of Educational Psychology, 77,</u> 631-645.

Gump, V.P. (1982). School settings and their keeping. In D. Duke (Ed.), <u>Helping teachers manage classrooms</u>. Alexandria, VA: Association for Supervision and Curriculum Development. (ERIC Document No. ED 218 710).

Guyton, E., & Hidalgo, F. (1995). Characteristics, responsibilities, and qualities of urban school mentors. <u>Education and Urban Society, 28</u> (1), 40-47.

Haberman, M. (1995). <u>Star teachers of children in poverty.</u> West Lafayette, IN: Kappa Delta Pi.

Hancock, V., & Betts, F. (1994). From the lagging to the leading edge. <u>Educational Leadership, 51</u> (7), 24-29.

Haycock, K. (1998, Summer). Good teaching matters…a lot. <u>Thinking K-16,</u> 3-16.

Hines, C.V., Cruickshank, D.R., & Kennedy, J.J. (1985). Teacher clarity and its relationship to student achievement and satisfaction. <u>American Educational Research Journal, 22</u> (1), 87-99.

Jordan, H.R., Mendro, R.L., & Weerasinghe, D. (1997, July). Teacher effects on longitudinal student achievement. Paper presented at the annual meeting of CREATE, Indianapolis, IN.

Karweit, N. (1988). Time-on-task: The second time around. <u>NASSP Bulletin, 72</u> (505), 31-39.

King, A. (1994). Guiding knowledge construction in the classroom: Effects of teaching children how to question and how to explain. <u>American Educational Research Journal, 31</u> (2), 338-368.

Knapp, M. S., Shields, P. M., & Turnbull, B. J. (1995). Academic challenge in high-poverty classrooms. <u>Phi Delta Kappan, 76</u> (10), 770-776.

Kounin, J.S. (1970). <u>Discipline and group management in classrooms.</u> Huntington, NY: Robert Krieger.

Kozma, R. (1982). Instructional design in a chemistry laboratory course: The impacts of structure and aptitudes on performance and attitudes. <u>Journal of Research in Science Teaching, 19</u> (3), 261-270.

Land, M.L. and Smith, L.R. (1979). Effect of a teacher clarity variable on student achievement. <u>Journal of Educational Research, 72</u> (4), 196-198.

Larrivee, B., & Algina, J. (1983, April). <u>Identification of teaching behaviors which predict success for mainstreamed students.</u> Paper presented at the annual meeting of the American Educational Research Association, Montreal, Canada. (ERIC Document Reproduction Service No. ED 232 362).

Lein, L., Johnson, J. F., & Ragland, M. (1997). <u>Successful Texas schoolwide programs: Research study results.</u> Austin, TX: The Charles Dana Center.

Little, J. W. (1982). Norms of collegiality and experimentation: Workplace conditions of school success. <u>American Educational Research Journal, 19</u> (3), 325-340.

Luiten, J.L., Ames, W., & Ackerman, C. (1980). Meta-analysis of the effects of advance organizers on learning and retention. <u>American Educational Research Journal, 17</u> (2), 211-218.

Manatt, R. P. (1994, July). How the School Improvement Model (SIM) uses evaluation to improve teaching and learning, paper presented at Third Annual National Evaluation Institute CREATE, Gatlingburg, TN.

Manatt, R. P., & Daniels, B. (1990). Relationships between principal ratings of teacher performance and student achievement. Journal of Personnel Evaluation in Education, 4,189-201.

Marshall, H. H. (1987). Motivational strategies of three fifth-grade teachers. The Elementary School Journal, 88, 135-150.

Marzano, R.J. (2003). What works in schools: Translating research into action. Alexandria, VA: Association for Supervision and Curriculum Development.

Marzano, R.J., Pickering, D.J., & Pollock, J.E. (2001). Classroom instruction that works: Research based strategies for increasing student achievement. Alexandria, VA: Association for Supervision and Curriculum Development.

McDonald, F. J. (1976). Research on teaching and its implications for policy malting: Resort on Phase II of the Beginning Teacher Evaluation Study. Princeton, NJ: Educational Testing Service.

McDonald, F.J. & Elias, P. (1976). The effects of teaching performance on pupil learning. Final Report No. 1. Beginning Teacher Evaluation Study, Phase II. Princeton, NJ: Educational Testing Service.

McMillan, J.H. (2000). Basic assessment concepts for teachers and administrators. Thousand Oaks, CA: Corwin Press.

Medley, D. (1977). Teacher competence and teacher effectiveness. Washinton, D.C.: American Association of Colleges for Teacher Education. (ERIC Document No. ED 143 629).

Medley, D. (1979). The effectiveness of teachers. In P. Peterson and H. Walberg (Eds.), Research on teaching: Concepts, findings, and implications. Berkeley, CA: McCutchan.

Mercado, C. I. (2001). The learner: "Race," "ethnicity," and linguistic difference. In V. Richardson (Ed.), Handbook of research on teaching (4th ed., pp. 668-964). Washington, DC: American Educational Research Association.

Morine-Dershimer, G. (1977). What's in a plan? Stated and unstated plans for lessons. Sacramento, CA: California State Commission for Teacher Preparation and Licensing. (ERIC Document No. ED 139 739).

Munby, H., Russell, T. & Marin, A. K. (2001). Teachers' knowledge and how it develops. In V. Richardson (Ed.), Handbook of research on teaching (4th ed., pp. 877-904). Washington, DC: American Educational Research Association.

Needels, M. & Stallings, J. (1975). Classroom processes related to absence rate. Menlo Park, CA: Stanford Research Institute.

Newby, T. J. (1991). Classroom motivation: Strategies of first-year teachers. Journal of Educational Psychology, 83, 195-200.

Noddings, N. (2001). The caring teacher. In V. Richardson (Ed.), Handbook of research on teaching (4th ed., pp. 99-105). Washington, DC: American Educational Research Association.

Norton, D. E. (1983). Through the eves of a child. Columbus, OH: Charles E. Merrill.

Okey, J., Capie, W., Ellett, C.D., and Johnson, C.E. (1978). Teacher performance validation studies. Paper presented at the annual meeting of the Georgia Educational Research Association.

O'Neil, J. (1992). Putting performance assessment to the test. Educational Leadership, 49 (8), 14-19.

Popham, W. J. (2001). The truth about testing: An educator's call to action. Alexandria, VA: Association for Supervision and Curriculum Development.

Porter, A. C., Youngs, P., & Odden, A. (2001). Advances in teacher assessments and their uses. In V. Richardson (Ed.), Handbook of research on teaching (4th ed., pp. 259-297). Washington, DC: American Educational Research Association.

Purkey, S. C., & Smith, M. S. (1983). Effective Schools: A review. The Elementary School Journal. 83 (4), 427-452.

Raymond, M., Fletcher, S. H., & Luque, J. (2001). Teach for America: An evaluation of teacher differences and student outcomes in Houston, Texas. Stanford, CA: Center for Research on Education Outcomes.

Redfield, D. L., & Rousseau, E. L. (1981). A meta-analysis of experimental research on teacher questioning behavior. Review of Educational Research, 51 (2), 237-245.

Reis, S. M., & Renzulli, J. S. (1992). Using curriculum compacting to challenge the above-average. Educational Leadership, 50 (2), 51-57.

Richardson, V. & Placier, P. (2001) Teacher change. In V. Richardson (Ed.), Handbook of research on teaching (4th ed., pp. 905-947). Washington, DC: American Educational Research Association.

Rivkin, S. G., Hanushek, E.A., & Kain, J. F. (2001). Teachers, schools, and academic achievement. Amherst, MA: Amherst College.

Rock, H. M., & Cummings, A. (1994). Can videodiscs improve student outcomes? Educational Leadership, 51 (7), 46-50.

Rosenshine, B. (1971). Teaching behaviors and student achievement. London: International Association for the Evaluation of Educational Achievement.

Rosenshine, B. (1983). Teaching functions in instructional programs. The Elementary School Journal, 83 (4), 335-351.

Rosenshine, B., & Berliner D. (1978). Academic engaged time. British Journal of Teacher Education, 4, 3-16.

Rowe, M.B. (1974). Wait-time and rewards as instructional variables, their influence on language, logic, and fate control: Part one, wait-time. Journal of Research in Science Teaching, 11 (2), 81-94.

Sanders, W. L. (1998, December). Value-added assessment. The school administrator, 24-27.

Sanders, W. L. & Rivers, J.C. (1996). Cumulative and residual effects of teachers on future student academic achievement. Knoxville, TN: University of Tennessee.

Sanford, J. P. and Evertson, C. M. (1980). Beginning the school year at a low SES junior high: Three case studies. Austin, X: The University of Texas, Research & Development Center for Teacher Evaluation. (ERIC Document No. ED 195 547).

Schmoker, M. (2001). The results fieldbook: Practical strategies from dramatically improved schools. Alexandria, VA: Association for Supervision and Curriculum Development.

Shepard, L. A. (2001). The role of classroom assessment in teaching and learning. In V. Richardson (Ed.), Handbook of research on teaching (4th ed., pp. 1066-1101). Washington, DC: American Educational Research Association.

Skinner, E. A., & Belmont (1993). Motivation in the classroom: Reciprocal effects of teacher behavior and student engagement across the school year. Journal of Educational Psychology, 85, 571-581.

Skinner, E. A., Wellborn, J. G., & Connell, J. P. (1990).What is takes to do well in school and whether I've got it. The role of perceived control in children's engagement and school achievement. Journal of Educational Psychology, 82, 616-622.

Smith, L.R. & Cotton, M.L. (1980). Effect of lesson vagueness and discontinuity on student achievement and attributes. Journal of Educational Psychology, 72 (5), 670-675.

Smith, L.R. & Edmonds, E.M. (1978). Teacher vagueness and pupil participation in mathematics learning. Journal for Research in Mathematics Education, 9 (3), 228-232.

Smith, L. R., & Sanders, K. (1981). The effects on student achievement of varying structure in social studies content. Journal of Educational Research, 74 (5), 333-336.

Soar, R.S. & Soar, R. M. (1972). An empirical analysis of selected Follow Through programs: An example of a process approach to evaluation. In I.J. Gordon et. al. (Eds.), Early childhood education. Chicago: National Society for the Study of Education.

Solomon, D., & Kendell, A. (1979). Children in classrooms: An investigation of person-environment interaction. New York: Praeger.

Southern Association on Children Under Six. (1990). Five Position Statements of the Southern Association on Children Under Six (SACUS). Little Rock, AR: Author.

Stallings, J. A. (1974). Follow through classroom observation evaluation 1972-1973— executive summary. (SRI Project URU-7370). Menlo Park, CA, Stanford Research Institute. (ERIC Document Reproduction Service No. ED 104 970).

Stallings, J.A. (1976). How instructional processes relate to child outcomes in a national study of Follow Through. Journal of Teacher Education, 27 (1), 43-47.

Stallings, J.A. (1978). Teaching basic reading skills in secondary schools. Toronto, Canada: American Educa-tional Research Association. (ERIC Document No. ED 166 634).

Stallings, J. A. (1981). What research has to say to administrators of secondary schools about effective teaching, and staff development. Menlo Park, CA: Stanford Research Institute. (ERIC Document Reproduction Service No. ED 209 748).

Stallings, J.A., Needels, M., & Stayrook, N. (1979). How to change the process of teaching basic reading skills in secondary schools. Menlo Park, CA: SRI International.

Taylor, A., & Valentine, B. (1985). Effective Schools. What research says about series. Number 1. data-search reports. Washington, D.C.: National Education Association. (ERIC Document Reproduction Service No. ED 274 073).

Wade, R. C. (1995). Encouraging student initiative in a fourth-grade classroom. The Elementary School Journal, 95, 339-354.

Wang, J. & Odell, S. J. (2002). Mentored learning to teach according to standards-based Reform: A critical review. Review of Educational Research, 72 (3), 481-546.

Wang, J. (2001). Contexts of mentoring and opportunities for learning to teach: A comparative study of mentoring practice. Teaching and Teacher Education, 17, 51-73.

Wayne, J. W. & Youngs, P (2003). Teacher characteristics and student achievement gains: A review. Review of Educational Research, 73 (1), 89-122.

Wharton-McDonald, R., Pressley, M. & Hampston, J. M. (1998, November). Literary instruction in nine first-grade classrooms: Teacher characteristics and student achievement. The Elementary School Journal, 101-128.

Wilson, E. A. (1996). Classroom management to encourage motivation and responsibility. Arlington, VA: Educational Research Service.

Wilson, S. M., & Berne, J. (1999). Teacher learning and the acquisition of professional knowledge: An examination of research on contemporary professional development. Review of Research in Education, 24, 173-209.

Woolfolk, A.E. & Brooks, D. M. (1983). Nonverbal communication in teaching. In E.W. Gordon (Ed.), Review of research in education, Vol. 10. Washington, D.C.: American Educational Research Association.

Wright, C.J. & Nuthall, G. (1970). Relationships between teacher behavior and pupil achievement in three experimental elementary science classes. American Educational Research Journal, 7 (4), 477-492.

Wright, S. P., Horn, S. P., & Sanders W. L. (1997, April). Teacher and classroom context effects on student achievement: Implications for teacher evaluation. Journal of Personnel Evaluation in Education, 57-67.

Wright, S. P., Horn, S. P., & Sanders, W. L. (1997). Teacher and classroom context effects on student achievement: Implications for teacher evaluation. Journal of Personnel Evaluation in Education, 11, 57-67.

Yap, K.O. & Enoki, D. Y. (1995). In search of the elusive magic bullet: Parental involvement and student outcomes. The School Community Journal, 5 (2), 97-106.